The Torts Game

DEFENDING MEAN JOE GREENE

The Torts Game

DEFENDING MEAN JOE GREENE

Jonathan L. Zittrain

Jack N. and Lillian R. Berkman Assistant Professor
for Entrepreneurial Legal Studies
Harvard Law School

Jennifer K. Harrison

Faegre & Benson LLP

ASPEN
PUBLISHERS

1185 Avenue of the Americas, New York, NY 10036
www.aspenpublishers.com

A Wolters Kluwer Company
www.aspenpublishers.com

Printed in the United States of America.

1 2 3 4 5 6 7 8 9 0

ISBN 0-7355-4509-X

Library of Congress Cataloging-in-Publication Data

Zittrain, Jonathan (Jonathan L.), 1969–
   The torts game : defending Mean Joe Greene / Jonathan Zittrain, Jennifer T.K. Harrison.
      p. cm.
   ISBN 0-7355-4509-X
   1. Torts–United States–Outlines, syllabi, etc. 2. Greene, Joe (Charles Edward)–Trials, litigation, etc. I. Harrison, Jennifer T.K., 1975- II. Title.

KF1250.Z9Z58 2004
346,7303–dc22

                                                    2004053121

About Aspen Publishers

Aspen Publishers, headquartered in New York City, is a leading information provider for attorneys, business professionals, and law students. Written by preeminent authorities, our products consist of analytical and practical information covering both U.S. and international topics. We publish in the full range of formats, including updated manuals, books, periodicals, CDs, and online products.

Our proprietary content is complemented by 2,500 legal databases, containing over 11 million documents, available through our Loislaw division. Aspen Publishers also offers a wide range of topical legal and business databases linked to Loislaw's primary material. Our mission is to provide accurate, timely, and authoritative content in easily accessible formats, supported by unmatched customer care.

To order any Aspen Publishers title, go to *www.aspenpublishers.com* or call 1-800-638-8437.

To reinstate your manual update service, call 1-800-638-8437.

For more information on Loislaw products, go to *www.loislaw.com* or call 1-800-364-2512.

For Customer Care issues, e-mail *CustomerCare@aspenpublishers.com*; call 1-800-234-1660; or fax 1-800-901-9075.

Aspen Publishers
A Wolters Kluwer Company

Summary of Contents

Contents

CHAPTER 1

CHAPTER 2

CHAPTER 3

THE MURKY LINE BETWEEN INTENTIONAL TORTS AND NEGLIGENCE

67

CHAPTER 4

VICARIOUS LIABILITY AND INTENTIONAL TORT

89

CHAPTER 5

INSURANCE: THE GAME BEHIND THE GAME

113

Preface

Like most of my colleagues, I teach torts from a casebook. Casebooks are, naturally enough, full of cases. These "cases" comprise a series of excerpts from judicial opinions — usually issued by appellate courts — that accompany holdings entered at just one moment in time within the life cycle of a given legal dispute. Most of the time that's a relief; both teachers and students would be overwhelmed trying to assimilate the full docket of a single typical case, much less the full range of activities that take place outside the courthouse records — phone calls, strategy sessions, negotiations, depositions. Judicial opinions are critical to learning and understanding the law, especially in a common law field such as torts, where there usually aren't statutes from which judges (and students) can draw guidance.

But I found that over the course of a first-year term, a certain unreality can set in precisely as the legal doctrines and surrounding arguments begin to feel natural. It becomes too easy to think of the practice of law as simply being a volley of arguments, followed by a glance to the judge to see whose barrage apparently scored more points. Law in general and litigation in particular are so much more than that: they entail strategizing and fencing and negotiation among real people, and even in the simplest cases such activities are rarely neatly divided between a single plaintiff and single defendant, each with neatly opposing interests.

Two years ago I shared with my students some tales and primary documents from a particular case not found in any casebook, not merely because it had yet to generate an appellate opinion but also because all of the interesting action took place nowhere near the courthouse. It turns out that almost all cases have this extra-judicial dimension, and once immersed in them, one finds their storylines and internal conflicts genuinely interesting — and relevant to an understanding of how the legal system actually works.

The materials were a success in class, and this book shares them. It offers a window into a single simple case, attempting to capture the realities of dealing with a lawsuit that stand apart from the doctrinal arguments that rightly consume most of a first-year law school curriculum, while also showing the mutual influence between those realities and the doctrinal questions that arise in a case.

This book would not have been possible without the generous cooperation and advice of those involved in the case, particularly Robert Berk and William Holm of Jones Skelton and Hochuli, P.L.C., Douglas C. Erikson of Maynard Cronin Erickson Curran & Sparks, P.L.C., my father, the late Lester E. Zittrain, who was for many years Joe Greene's personal attorney, and Charles "Mean Joe" Greene. Practitioners within the local Pennsylvania and Kansas legal communities offered their own helpful impressions of the case early in the book's drafting: Daniel Berger, James Croshal, Kate Fagan, Nora Berry Fischer, Gayle Godfrey, Foster Goldman, Jack Kunz, Michael Louik, Merle Mermelstein, Dave Rebein, Phil Ridenour, Trip Sawver, Tim Schweers, Seymour Sikov, Bill Skepnek, Bill Tighe, Stacey Vernallis, Marie Williams, and Wendel Wurst. Harvard Law School students Erika Reinders, Greg Skidmore, and Betsy Zedek performed excellent research assistance for later drafts of the book — including forays to the Saval Insurance Education Center run by the Insurance Library Association of Boston. And heartfelt thanks are due to Professor Kenneth Abraham of the University of Virginia School of Law for offering his wisdom on the current state of insurance law.

Both Jennifer Harrison and I were grounded in — and taught to love — the law at early ages by our parents, she by her father, K. Mike Kimball, of the Kimball Law Firm, and I by my father and mother, Lester E. Zittrain and Ruth A. Zittrain, of Zittrain & Zittrain. (Neither ever said which comes first in the firm's title.) It is to our parents that this book is dedicated with love and thanks.

Jonathan Zittrain
July 2004

THE ROSTER

Offense

Mark Cockriel – Plaintiff; sound engineer struck by Joe Greene
    Douglas Erickson – Mark Cockriel's attorney
    Mark Baldree, Charles Meinstin, and Bonnie Quinn – Medical experts listed
        for the plaintiff

Defense

Charles E. "Mean Joe" Greene – Defendant; Arizona Cardinals defensive line coach
    Lester E. Zittrain – Joe Greene's personal attorney
    Farmers Insurance – Mean Joe Greene's homeowners insurer
        Ken Sanders – Branch Claims Manager, Farmers Insurance
            Company of Arizona
        James R. Broening – Attorney retained by Farmers Insurance

Arizona Cardinals – Defendant; National Football League team
    Michael K. Kennedy and Shannon Clark – Attorneys for the Arizona Cardinals
    Michael Bidwell – Vice President and General Counsel of the Arizona Cardinals;
        deposed by the defense
    David McGinnis – Head Coach of the Arizona Cardinals;
        deposed by the defense
    Gulf/Select Insurance – Arizona Cardinals' primary insurer
        Beverly Miller – Claims Manager for Select Insurance, a Gulf subsidiary
        Robert "Bob" Berk and William "Bill" Holm – Attorneys retained by
            Gulf Insurance to defend Joe Greene

Referee

Judge William L. Topf – Trial judge

Spectators

Randall Robert "Randy" Piotroski – Sound engineer who witnessed the incident;
    deposed by the plaintiff
Ray Hamilton – Defensive Line Coach of the New England Patriots
    at the time of the incident

1

THE INCIDENT BEHIND THE CASE

Greene admits hitting worker after game

By Lee Shappell
The Arizona Republic

Cardinals defensive line coach Joe Greene acknowledged Monday that he hit a worker who had driven over his foot with a flatbed golf cart on the Sun Devil Stadium field after a 27-3 loss to New England on Sunday.

Joe Greene

Greene apologized to the Cardinals and to Coach Vince Tobin for any embarrassment the incident caused them.

"Normally after a ballgame I'm pretty quick off the field," Greene said. "On this particular occasion, I just sat on the bench. Like most of the people in the organization, I was depressed."

Greene said he spotted a coaching acquaintance from the Patriots leaving the field and got up to try to catch up to him.

"I lost him in the crowd, I was looking over the top, and I walked right next to the buggy or whatever this thing was," said Greene, who earned induction into the Pro Football Hall of Fame after his playing days with the Pittsburgh Steelers. "I stopped. I said, 'What are you going to do, run over me?'

"He looked at me and proceeded to run over my foot and I slapped him. End of story."

The driver of the cart, Mark Cockriel, 45, said Greene's blow knocked his glasses off his face. Cockriel was working in the crew setting up a portable stage for a post-game concert by swing band Big Bad Voodoo Daddy.

Cardinals Coach Vince Tobin said he planned no disciplinary action against Greene.

"I would have to think that something would have to be proven one way or the other," Tobin said. "I don't know who was at fault or who was not at fault. I don't think I can be judge and jury of something I didn't see. I wasn't there. I talked to Joe about it. I believe what Joe told me."

Greene said he wouldn't know Cockriel again if he saw him.

"If the exchange would have been, 'Sorry, I didn't see you,' and 'Sorry, I didn't see you, either,' then it would have been over," said Greene, who appeared to be walking normally. "It happened just that quickly. I used profanity when I said, 'Are you going to run over me?' He just looked at me and he started up again.

"In terms of my reactions I stand up to those, good or bad."

Cockriel had a welt above his left cheek. He was treated by Cardinals medical personnel.

The news story above presents a first view of the facts of the case explored in this book. Of course, the newspaper's version of the facts is likely to differ greatly from one or several of the parties' versions of the facts. Mark Cockriel, the sound engineer who was struck by Joe Greene, might describe the incident as follows:[1]

I work as a sound engineer, and part of my job is to set up sound equipment for concerts. On October 31, 1999, I was at the Sun Devil Stadium after a Cardinals

---

[1] This is not a narrative ever voiced by Mark Cockriel; rather, the authors created the description from the pleadings filed in the subsequent lawsuit.

football game to set up for a concert. I was driving a cart pulling some sound equipment on to the field. There were lots of people around. There were quite a few fans and other people still there from the football game at that time, including some members of the media. I had to keep stopping when pedestrians would get in the way of the cart. One of the band's roadies was in the trailer I was pulling behind the cart to make sure the equipment traveled safely.

As I was driving the cart on the field, "Mean Joe" Greene, who is one of the assistant coaches for the Cardinals football team, was also crossing the field. Our paths crossed, and I stopped the cart to avoid running into him. He glared at me and then, among other things, yelled, "What the fuck were you going to do, run over me?!?" He basically dared me to move the cart, so I did drive forward a little bit. The wheels of the cart might have touched his foot or something, but I'm not sure. Then he hit me really hard on the side of the head. He hit me so hard that my glasses flew into the air a long way. (My glasses were later found in the end zone, and this happened at about the 10 yard line.) After he hit me, Joe just walked off the field.

Right after he hit me, it hurt really badly and I had some swelling on my head, the side of my face, and my neck, and my ears were ringing. I was treated on the scene by a Cardinals medic but all he gave me was some Advil. I did continue to work that concert and didn't miss any concerts after that. But the ringing in my ears didn't go away (in fact, I had ringing in my ears for several months). As a sound engineer, it is really important that I have good hearing, and it doesn't make life very easy to have ringing in my ears all the time. I went to a doctor, which cost $285. It turns out I had a punctured ear drum and some hearing loss, although the ringing has stopped and I can hear fine now.

I want to sue Mean Joe Greene for what he did to me.

Joe Greene was interviewed by his defense attorneys as they prepared to negotiate, and potentially litigate, on his behalf. The following memorandum summarizes Joe's description of the facts as he remembered them on the day of the interview.

JONES, SKELTON & HOCHULI, P.L.C.

MEMORANDUM

TO: File

FROM: RRB

DATE: July 14, 2000

SUBJECT: Cockriel v. Joe Greenee

I spoke today to our client, Joe Greene, regarding the events in question. Mr. Greene stated that the incident occurred after the Arizona Cardinals v. New England Patriots game on October 31, 1999. He stated that his usual practice at the end of games is to immediately run down the sidelines and into the tunnel. At the end of the Patriots game, however, he sat on the team bench for between two and five minutes. He explained that it was a long, grueling game, that his hip and back hurt and that he needed to rest for a few minutes. He also suggested that he was very upset by the loss.

After resting for a few minutes, Mr. Greene ran diagonally across the field toward the goal post. He explained that the reason he ran onto the field instead of down the sidelines was because he wanted to catch up with, and congratulate, the defensive line coach for the New England Patriots.

As Mr. Greene was partially across the field, looking for the opposing defensive line coach among the many people on the field, he was almost run over by a small vehicle/cart. He stated that had he not stopped abruptly, the cart would have hit him. According to Mr. Greene, he looked at the driver and said: "What the fuck are you going to do, run over me?" He stated that the driver looked at him for a few seconds, and then proceeded forward, running over Mr. Greene's foot. Mr. Greene stated there was no question in his mind but that the driver either intentionally ran over his foot or consciously disregarded the likelihood that he would run over Mr. Greene's foot.

File
RRB
July 14, 2000
Cockreil v. Joe Green

Page 2

According to Mr. Greene, either while the vehicle was still on his foot or immediately it drove over his foot, he reached across and slapped the driver in the face. His best guess is that he hit the driver, Mr. Cockriel, on the cheek, and he recalls that one of his fingers hit Mr. Cockriel's glasses and knocked them off. Mr. Greene stated that after he struck Mr. Cockriel, Mr. Cockriel asked, "Why did you do that?" and Mr. Greene's response was: "You ran over my foot."

Mr. Greene stated that he struck Mr. Cockriel with an open hand, and that although he knocked Mr. Cockriel's glasses off, Mr. Cockriel remained in the cart. After the slap, Mr. Cockriel drove away, and Mr. Greene does not know if he left the field or if he proceeded to do whatever he was on the field to do (presumably to set up a post-game concert).

Mr. Greene does not have any personal knowledge of what Mr. Cockriel did after the incident, and he never saw or spoke to Mr. Cockriel again. He was later told by the Cardinals' team doctor, however, that the doctor examined Mr. Cockriel after the incident and found no injuries other than a welt on Mr. Cockriel's face. Mr. Greene stated that he did not know how he might have damaged Mr. Cockriel's eardrum when he never struck Mr. Cockriel's ear.

A few other points. First, Mr. Greene stated that when he first confronted the vehicle driven by Mr. Cockriel, it was something of a stand-off. He explained that unless either he moved or Mr. Cockriel steered away, there was going to be a collision. Second, Mr. Greene stated that Mr. Cockriel never gave him an opportunity to move out of the way, and that immediately after Mr. Greene said: "What the fuck are you going to do, run over me?", Mr. Cockriel ran over him. Third, Mr. Greene recalls smelling beer at the time of the incident. He is not sure whether the smell was coming from Mr. Cockriel, or whether it was from other people on the field or in the stands.

Legal action often does not begin with the filing of a lawsuit. Instead, an aggrieved party's lawyer may send a written notice demanding some action by the would-be defendant. Depending on the nature of a potential plaintiff's claim, a demand letter could ask the would-be defendant for any combination of paying money to the claimant, ceasing an objectionable activity, or performing a previously promised task. Most demand letters contain the following elements: a description of the plaintiff and the harm suffered by him or her at the hands of the defendant, an offer to settle for a specified amount, and a deadline for acceptance of the settlement offer. The following demand letter, sent by Mark Cockriel's attorney to the Cardinals' (Joe Greene's employer's) counsel, was the first volley in a suit by Mark against Joe.

April 14, 2000

Michael K. Kennedy, Esq.
Gallagher & Kennedy
2600 North Central Avenue
Phoenix, Arizona 85004-3050

　　　Re:　*Mark Cockriel adv. Arizona Cardinals/"Mean Joe" Greene*

Dear Mr. Kennedy:

　　　　　This letter is intended to fall within the scope of Rule 408, Arizona Rules of Evidence, in that it proposes a compromise or settlement of certain claims relating to the actions and negligence of the Arizona Cardinals and Charles Edward Greene.　We address this letter to you because it is our understanding that you will represent one or more of the adverse parties, if this matter proceeds to litigation.

　　　　　As you know, an employee of the Arizona Cardinals, Charles Edwards Greene (a/k/a "Mean Joe Greene") assaulted Mark Cockriel on October 31,1999.　An assault, for purposes of establishing criminal liability in Arizona is defined as:

　　　　　　　1. Intentionally, knowingly or recklessly causing any
　　　　　　　physical injury to another person;　or

　　　　　　　2. Intentionally placing another person in reasonable
　　　　　　　apprehension of imminent physical injury;　or

　　　　　　　3. Knowingly touching another person with the intent
　　　　　　　to injure, insult or provoke such person.

A.R.S. § 13-1203.　In addition, where an assault causes serious physical injury, the law deems it an "aggravated" assault.　*See* A.R.S. § 13-1204(A).

Michael K. Kennedy, Esquire
April 14, 2000
Page 2

For purposes of establishing a civil cause of action, a plaintiff typically would show:

An actor is subject to liability to another for battery if

(a)   he acts intending to cause a harmful or offensive contact with the person of the other or a third person, or an imminent apprehension of such a contact, and

(b)   a harmful contact with the person of the other directly or indirectly results.

Restatement (Second) of Torts, § 13 (as to a "battery"). Alternatively,

An actor is subject to liability to another for assault if

(a)   he acts intending to cause a harmful or offensive contact with the person of the other or a third person, or an imminent apprehension of such a contact, and

(b)   the other is thereby put in such imminent apprehension.

Restatement (Second) of Torts, § 21 (as to an "assault").

On November 12, 1999, at your request, we furnished to you a video tape of this incident. The tape is provocative and clear with respect to the events. Any suggestion that Mr. Greene's assault was a reaction to his foot being run over by a cart, as he may have suggested to the media, is clearly belied by the tape. In addition, several members of the press were standing nearby when the attack took place and will refute such a scenario. Legally, however, even if his toe had been touched by a tire, that fact would not constitute a defense to a cause of action.

Michael K. Kennedy, Esquire
April 14, 2000
Page 3

I am preparing a draft complaint and notice of deposition for Mr. Greene. In short order, if a civil action were filed, we would notice or move the court for leave to notice other representatives of ownership and management who would be expected to have relevant information. We also will be requesting extensive background materials on Mr. Greene and thoroughly review the circumstances under which he was hired, management's knowledge of his character and history, his reputation in the profession, as well as the precise style and scope of the Cardinal's supervision of Mr. Greene.

As you may know, Mr. Cockriel is an educated and highly qualified sound engineer. As one might then expect, his most precious sense is his hearing. Following this incident, Cardinal physician, Dr. Wayne Kuhl, treated Mr. Cockriel with Advil. In reality, Mr. Cockriel's eardrum was ruptured, resulting in significant pain, loss of hearing, and considerable apprehension over the prospect of losing not only his hearing, but also his career and the business he built in the industry. We have enclosed medical records reflecting his post-incident treatment, assessment, and, fortunately, his recovery. While he is thankful to have made an apparent full recovery, the anxiety during the four months before it could be determined that his prognosis was positive, was grueling. Unfortunately, the embarrassment and humiliation of being assaulted by a celebrity in front of literally thousands of people continues.

The Restatement of Torts recognizes that conduct which is extreme and outrageous may cause severe emotional distress for which one may be subject to liability. Restatement (Second) of Torts § 46(1) (1965). The Restatement also states that the tort of emotional distress inflicted intentionally or recklessly is recognized as a separate and distinct basis of tort liability. There is no need to show elements of other torts such as assault and battery. Restatement (Second) of Torts § 46 comment b (1965). A comment to § 46 states that there is liability: where the conduct has been so outrageous in character, and so extreme in degree, as to go beyond all possible bounds of decency, and to be regarded as atrocious, and utterly intolerable in a civilized community. . . in which . . . an average member of the community would . . . exclaim,

Michael K. Kennedy, Esquire
April 14, 2000
Page 4

"Outrageous!" <u>Id</u>. comment d. We have followed this
standard for liability.

<u>Ford v. Revlon</u>, 153 Ariz. 38, 43, 734 P.2d 580, 585 (1987).

In addition to claims for assault, battery, emotional distress,
negligent hiring and negligent supervision, the theory of punitive damages
seems particularly appropriate here. What may be difficult to gauge is the
amount of money as to a celebrity like Mr. Greene and a multimillion dollar
empire like the Cardinals a jury would consider adequate to punish egregious
conduct and deter such conduct in the future. We suspect that amount would
be substantial.

Mr. Cockriel has instructed me to file a complaint on May 1, 2000,
unless his grievance can be resolved prior to that time. In order for a settlement
to be reached, payment in the amount of $100,000.00 must be received in this
office by 5:00 p.m. on April 28, 2000. Mr. Cockriel also expects a written
apology from Mr. Greene. If the Cardinals and Mr. Greene are not interested in
a pre-litigation resolution, I would appreciate your advising me as to whether you
will be authorized to accept service for either party and advising your clients that
Mr. Greene's deposition will be noticed for Thursday, July 6, 2000 at 10:00 a.m,
so we can avoid scheduling conflicts.

Very truly yours,

Douglas C. Erickson

Not all demand letters are as lengthy and intricate as the one sent to the
Cardinals' counsel by Mark's attorney. Some, seeking simply to draw the would-be
defendant into negotiations, may not even specify a sum.

QUESTIONS

1. Why did Doug Erickson send a demand letter to the Cardinals discussing
   assault, battery, and emotional distress when it was Joe's actions that caused the
   alleged assault, battery, and emotional distress? Why might the Cardinals be
   liable for the individual actions of one of its employees?
2. How directly are the facts as related by the newspaper story, Joe, and Mark in
   direct conflict?
3. How might one calculate damages in this kind of case? What percentage of
   Mark's damages likely reflects the hard costs of medical treatment and recovery

and what percentage reflects recoverable intangibles such as humiliation and pain and suffering?

The newspaper account, Joe's lawyer's write-up of Joe's view of the story, and Mark's demand letter provide a flavor of the incident giving rise to a claim for damages — and a foundation for examining how an incident such as this one can be portrayed as intentional wrongdoing, negligence, or a wholly innocent, if unfortunate, encounter. The rest of this book examines how the case progressed, with emphasis on the strategic decisions that faced lawyers on what would quickly turn out to be more than two sides.

2

LAWYERING THE FACTS

THE BASICS

Assault (§ 21)

(1) An actor is subject to liability to another for assault if
    (a) he acts intending to cause a harmful or offensive contact with the person of the other or a third person, or an imminent apprehension of such a contact, and
    (b) the other is thereby put in such imminent apprehension.
(2) An action which is not done with the intention stated in Subsection (1, a) does not make the actor liable to the other for an apprehension caused thereby although the act involves an unreasonable risk of causing it and, therefore, would be negligent or reckless if the risk threatened bodily harm.

Restatement (Second) of Torts § 21 (1965).

Battery (§ 13)

An actor is subject to liability to another for battery if
    (a) he acts intending to cause a harmful or offensive contact with the person of the other or a third person, or an imminent apprehension of such a contact, and
    (b) a harmful contact with the person of the other directly or indirectly results.

Restatement (Second) of Torts § 13 (1965).

Law students are often surprised by how difficult it is to find a clear statement of the law in a law school casebook. Casebooks rarely include Restatement[1] sections or jury instructions setting forth the doctrinal elements of a tort, but instead focus on the interesting cases at the edges of the doctrine. Indeed, it would be difficult to create a casebook of open and shut cases, as such cases are not the stuff of appellate opinions. By definition, recorded appellate opinions describe cases in which there was some dispute over the way the law should be applied in a matter.

In the world outside of law school casebooks, however, many cases do seem clear-cut. Upon reading the facts in the first chapter about the incident between Joe and Mark, one might wonder how an entire book could be built around such a clear-cut assault and battery claim. How does a lawyer respond when faced with a seemingly clear-cut case? Sometimes the sensible thing to do is settle — attempt to negotiate an agreement to end the case. A plaintiff might agree to settle even with a strong case to avoid the expense and trouble of litigation — which even for simple incidents can unfold over a period of months or years.

---

[1] A Restatement is a resource created by law professors that attempts to craft general rules from case law research. A Restatement is sometimes a good place to start research, but never a good place to end it. It is important to be careful not to rely on Restatement sections, because the statements have no binding effect in court. Indeed, the law in a particular jurisdiction may diverge from the Restatement rule. In some areas of law, the case law is so conflicting and confused that the Restatement provides no real help even as a starting point. For assault and battery, however, the Restatement provides convenient shorthand with which to begin an analysis.

As Chapter 1 suggested, the facts may not be entirely clear. Assault and battery and associated defenses can depend in part on motive, and a newspaper story is a thin substitute for the materials rigorously accreted in the course of actual preparation for litigation. Further, if other defendants are to be targeted beyond Joe, additional facts will have to be shown. For the Cardinals to be responsible, Joe's relationship to them and other context will have to be developed, as we will see in Chapter 4. If there is hope of insurance company involvement — something that both defendants and plaintiff could want — the intentional nature of Mark's claims may have to be down-played, for reasons we will explore in Chapter 3. (Chapter 5 covers the truly fascinating situations that can arise as insurance companies square off against their own insureds precisely when they believe the facts excuse coverage — yet when the facts have not been formally and fully developed.)

Before trial, lawyers use information-gathering tools such as depositions to investigate the facts. Depositions are essentially interviews of parties, witnesses, and other relevant persons taken under oath and recorded. Lawyers use depositions not only to ascertain an opponent's story, but also to begin developing the fact record and legal arguments the lawyer will ultimately put before the jury. Attorneys for all of the parties are typically present at a deposition, and may make objections on the record for later review by the judge. A judge is not present at depositions except in special circumstances, and depositions themselves are admissible at trial only for limited purposes. Typically, a deponent must give testimony all over again, live in the courtroom, if a case should proceed to trial and the deponent's answers are deemed relevant to the trial.

The lawyers in this case took the depositions of Joe, Mark, and others to elicit their observations surrounding the incident, and such important issues as the relationship between Joe and the Cardinals. This chapter's readings are primarily drawn from transcripts of those depositions. The same features that make depositions naturally voluminous — they're raw transcripts of conversations rather than edited documents — make them quick reads. The excerpts we offer here show the degree to which each side is to accept at face value the facts as relayed in the newspaper article that opened Chapter 1. The first excerpt reproduced below is from Mark's attorney's deposition of Joe. (Joe's legal name is Charles E. Greene, and the deposition is in that name.) We offer a few questions to briefly think about before you read the excerpts; you can then compare your own strategy to that employed by the lawyers.

QUESTIONS

1. If you were Joe's lawyer, what key issues would you expect to arise during the deposition? How would you prepare your client to respond to those questions?
2. If you represented Mark, what would you like Joe to admit during the deposition? What would your strategy be to elicit those admissions?

Our excerpt begins mid-stream:

1   [LAWYER] And you understand that that is what

2   this lawsuit is about, correct?

3   [GREENE] I understand that is -- that is what

4   this is about? Not really.

5   Q. Do you recall the event that we're

6   talking about?

7   A. Yes.

8   Q. Tell me, as best you can recall, how

9   that event occurred.

10   A. Well, to the best of my ability, what

11   happened, and I think it was in October of '99,

12   we had -- we were playing -- we had just

13   finished playing -- pardon me. We had just

14   finished getting beaten up pretty badly by the

15   New England Patriots, and it was a very

16   disappointing outing.

17   I have a friend that I -- that I

18   played ball against, and he coaches defensive

19   line in the National Football League, and so do

20   I. So we talk about players and our ups and

21   downs in the league.

22   But anyway, he was on the -- he

23   coached for the New England Patriots. And if we

24   could use this table as a football field, I'm on

25   the -- this side here. He's on the opposite

CHARLES E. GREENE   11/03/2000

42

```
 1   side.  Our locker rooms -- our locker rooms are

 2   in the same direction.  They're at the end zone

 3   end.  I don't know if it's -- what is it, the

 4   west end?  Yeah, whatever.

 5              And when the game was over, as it's

 6   customary, I -- I -- I'm off the field.  But

 7   for some reason, this time I -- I was tired,

 8   disgusted, disappointed, and I sat down on the

 9   bench, rested my feet.

10              And then I thought about Ray, and I

11   said, well, let me go say hello to Ray because

12   he'll think I'm sour grapes because they beat up

13   on us.  So I saw him.  They were -- he was in

14   the middle of the field.  These guys were doing

15   their prayer ceremony.

16              So I saw him, and as I was walking, I

17   was going to meet him halfway.  That's what I

18   was -- caught myself doing.  He was coming

19   across the field, and I was going to meet him

20   right there.

21              And as I was looking through the crowd,

22   I lost him.  And I kept looking at him.  And

23   somewhere, probably around, I'm guessing, maybe

24   the 20 yard line, about near the hash mark, I

25   walked up on the gentleman in some form of cart,
```

1   and he -- didn't see him. I didn't know if he

2   saw me.

3   And as -- I mean, I got -- I was

4   right there on him, and I put my hand on the

5   vehicle to keep from falling over the vehicle.

6   And I said, well, you know, what are you going to

7   do, run over me? And I -- I cursed.

8   And he looked at me just like you're

9   looking at me, looked at me, and proceeded to

10   roll over my foot. And as he was probably on top

11   of my foot or coming off my foot, somewhere in

12   there, I reacted, I slapped him.

13   Q. Anything else you recall about the

14   event itself?

15   A. That's it. He rode away. Well, his

16   glasses came off. He said, what did you do that

17   for? I said, you rolled over my foot. I think

18   his -- some guy that was on the thing with him

19   sweared at me, and I -- I walked off.

20   Q. Who was the acquaintance that you were

21   going to meet, Ray?

22   A. He coaches for the -- he coached for

23   the New England Patriots.

24   Q. What was his last name?

25   A. I'm telling you his name was Ray.

CHARLES E. GREENE   11/03/2000

44

1	Q. Sir, do you know his last name?
2	A. I'll remember it sometime later on
3	maybe.
4	Q. You indicated that you were going to
5	meet Ray, I believe you said halfway. Where did
6	you envision on the field actually meeting up
7	with him?
8	A. Well, I was just going to cross paths
9	with him. I said I was sitting -- my bench was
10	here. Theirs was over there. And I saw him in
11	the middle of the field, and they were having
12	this prayer ceremony, as players do, I guess,
13	after the ballgame. Opposing players come
14	together, and they pray for one another.
15	And I saw him, and then I lost him in
16	the crowd. And I was looking over the crowd,
17	searching for him, and I was drifting across the
18	field.
19	I was going to probably meet him
20	somewhere between, you know, the field and the
21	locker room. And that's what I chose to do. You
22	know, normally -- normally I'm off the field. I
23	don't -- you know, at any rate, as I was looking
24	over the top of the field, looking for Ray, I
25	walked up on the cart.

CHARLES E. GREENE   11/03/2000

45

```
 1         Q.  So I take it you didn't see the cart
 2    approaching you?
 3         A.  No.
 4         Q.  And the reason you didn't see it was
 5    because you were looking, trying to look above
 6    the crowd to see Ray?
 7         A.  Right.
 8         Q.  And the reason that you weren't off the
 9    field right away on this particular occasion is
10    because you just suffered such a bad defeat?
11         A.  It was disappointing.  Yeah, it was.  I
12    was feeling sorry for myself.
13         Q.  You were discouraged?
14         A.  Feeling sorry for myself.
15         Q.  And was there something in particular
16    about the way the defense played that day that
17    was particularly upsetting?
18         A.  Oh, no.  It's -- I think we got beat
19    31 to nothing or 38 to nothing or something like
20    that.  It was bad.  It was just, it was poor.  It
21    was a poor, poor performance, and it was -- it
22    was disappointing.  It was disappointing, very
23    disappointing.
24         Q.  Do you recall what the Cardinals'
25    record was after that game?
```

CHARLES E. GREENE   11/03/2000
46

1   A.   No. It probably wasn't good, but I
2   don't recall.
3   Q.   When you first saw the cart that
4   Mr. Cockriel was driving, was it stopped or
5   moving?
6   A.   Stopped.
7   Q.   And it was --
8   A.   Right there, it was stopped. I don't
9   know if it was moving prior to. I can't tell you
10   that. I know I put my hand down.
11   Q.   Did you put your hand down after you
12   first saw the cart?
13   A.   After? You know, I don't -- I
14   couldn't tell you. I just, it was a reaction
15   that there was something there, that I was about
16   to get hit. And I put my -- I put my hand on it
17   to keep from -- I think it probably -- I'm not
18   sure. I couldn't tell you whether it was rolling
19   or not. Honestly, I just couldn't tell you
20   that. I just reacted, and I know that when my
21   hand was there, it wasn't moving.
22   Q.   And the reason you put your hand out on
23   the cart was so that you wouldn't fall over the
24   cart, is that right?
25   A.   I put my hand on the cart so that I

CHARLES E. GREENE　　11/03/2000

47

```
1  wouldn't get hit.  That was my thought at the
2  time.
3       Q.  And when you put your hand on the cart,
4  the cart was not moving?
5       A.  I know that when my hand was on the
6  cart, the cart was still.
7       Q.  And at that point in time, you had a
8  verbal exchange with the driver, Mr. Cockriel?
9       A.  Right.
10       Q.  And you asked him about was he going to
11  run you over or something to that effect?
12       A.  Right.  Correct.
13       Q.  And did he respond to you verbally?
14       A.  No.  He looked at me.
15       Q.  I know, like I'm looking at you.
16       A.  Right.
17       Q.  You don't recall any verbal response by
18  him?
19       A.  No.  He didn't -- he didn't -- he
20  didn't say anything.
21       Q.  And after you make those comments to
22  him or ask him that question, then he starts the
23  vehicle again and runs over your foot?
24       A.  Right.  Correct.
25       Q.  And at that point in time, you hit
```

```
 1  him?
 2        A.  I slapped him.
 3        Q.  Why did you do that?
 4        A.  At the time it was just a spontaneous
 5  reaction, spontaneous reaction.
 6        Q.  Do you recall being angry?
 7        A.  No.  I wasn't angry.  I wasn't angry.
 8  As I said, the mood that I was in was one of
 9  sorrow, disappointment.
10        Q.  Do you -- I'm sorry.  Were you done?
11        Do you recall being -- well, I take it
12  you weren't fearful for your life, were you?
13        A.  That would be an exaggeration.
14        Q.  Were you fearful for your well-being?
15        MR. BERK:  Form.
16        MR. CLARK:  Join.
17        THE WITNESS:  I don't know what would
18  have happened to me had the -- the cart run over
19  me.  I don't know.  You know, I'm -- at the time
20  I'm -- I was 53 years old.  I've been -- I've
21  been -- I played football for 13 years.  I
22  got -- I got bruises.  I got bad hips, bad
23  elbows, bad shoulders, bad feet from standing on
24  the field for 30 minutes.
25        There's a lot of, you know, creaking
```

CHARLES E. GREENE   11/03/2000

1   going on when I'm moving. So if the cart would

2   have hit me, I don't know what would have

3   happened. And I can't say, you know, what would

4   have happened then. I just don't know.

5   And I can't tell you that I was in fear

6   of my life. No, I wasn't in fear of my life. I

7   didn't want to get hit by the cart.

8   Q. (BY MR. ERICKSON) At the time that you

9   had that exchange with Mr. Cockriel, you were

10   actually standing beside the cart, isn't that

11   correct?

12   A. I was -- I was on the -- I was

13   probably on the front right wheel, somewhere in

14   that vicinity.

15   Q. You weren't actually in front of the

16   cart, were you?

17   A. Not in front of the cart. Just to the

18   edge of the cart. Probably to the edge of it,

19   the edge or the front. More -- I would probably

20   have to say more -- if I would have to pick a

21   direction, it was probably more to the side, near

22   the front.

23   Q. So if the cart had continued on the

24   path that it was on at that point in time, it

25   would not have run you over, correct?

CHARLES E. GREENE   11/03/2000

50

1   A.   No.   How do you come to that

2   conclusion?

3   Q.   Well, I'm asking you.

4   A.   I don't think so.

5   Q.   You don't think the cart would have run

6   you over, or you think the cart would have run

7   you over?

8   A.   I don't think it's coming from the

9   direction where you're coming from.   I'm

10 believing what you're saying.   That's what I'm

11 saying.

12   Q.   So it's your recollection that if the

13 cart had continued on in the direction it was

14 moving, it would have run you over?

15   A.   Probably because my -- as I said, my

16 foot, I'm -- I'm standing right there in front

17 of, near the front of the cart.   I did not move.

18 And when I said, what are you going to do, run

19 over me and, again, I -- I cursed, when I said

20 it, and he looked at me, there it is, and rolled

21 right over my foot.

22   I did not move.   I didn't do anything.

23 He didn't veer.   I was there.   And the words

24 really barely got out of my mouth, looked at me

25 and went just like that (indicating).

CHARLES E. GREENE   11/03/2000

51

1   Q.   If your recollection is correct and

2   after this conversation he started the cart again

3   and then it rolled over your foot, why was your

4   foot in a position to be rolled over at that

5   point?

6   MR. BERK: Form.

7   MR. CLARK: Join.

8   THE WITNESS: Because that's -- that's

9   where I was when I put my hand over and asked the

10 question.

11   Q.   (BY MR. ERICKSON)   Did you hit

12 Mr. Cockriel because you thought it would stop

13 him from running you over?

14   A.   No.

15   Q.   Why did you hit Mr. Cockriel?

16   A.   I responded with a slap to the face

17 because he ran over my foot.   He was on top of my

18 foot, probably leaving my foot, when I

19 instinctively struck him with my palm.

20   Q.   You did intend to hit him, correct?

21   MR. BERK: Form.

22   MR. CLARK: Join.

23   THE WITNESS: It wasn't planned.

24   Q.   (BY MR. ERICKSON)   I'm not asking you

25 whether it was planned.   I'm asking you whether

CHARLES E. GREENE   11/03/2000

1 you intentionally hit Mr. Cockriel?

2   MR. BERK: Form.

3   MR. CLARK: Join.

4   THE WITNESS: I -- I can say I did not

5 intend not to hit him.

6   Q. (BY MR. ERICKSON) It wasn't an

7 accident that you happened to make contact with

8 his head, was it?

9   MR. BERK: Form.

10   MR. CLARK: Join.

11   THE WITNESS: Would it be an accident

12 if he ran over my foot?

13   Q. (BY MR. ERICKSON) Can you answer my

14 question?

15   MR. BERK: If you can answer it

16 differently than you already answered it, go

17 ahead.

18   THE WITNESS: No. No. Now we're just

19 jostling. No.

20   MR. ERICKSON: Would you read my

21 question back, please?

22   (The record was read by the reporter as

23 requested.)

24   Q. (BY MR. ERICKSON) Can you answer that

25 question?

CHARLES E. GREENE   11/03/2000

53

1	MR. BERK: Form.

1   MR. BERK: Form.

2   MR. CLARK: Again, join.

3   THE WITNESS: What did I -- did I --

4 did I answer that before?

5   Q. (BY MR. ERICKSON) No, sir. You asked

6 me whether it would be an accident if he ran over

7 your foot.

8   MR. BERK: I think you have already

9 answered it. So if you can't answer it better

10 than you've already answered it, I'm not going to

11 make you answer it again. You tell him whether

12 you can answer it differently.

13   THE WITNESS: I don't think so. No. I

14 slapped him when he was on top of my foot,

15 probably when he was leaving, spontaneous

16 reaction.

17   Q. (BY MR. ERICKSON) Did you intend to

18 hit him?

19   MR. BERK: Don't answer it again. You

20 don't have to answer that question.

21   MR. ERICKSON: You're instructing him

22 not to answer?

23   MR. BERK: It's harassment at that

24 point. He answered it was spontaneous. I don't

25 know whether that's intentional or accidental.

CHARLES E. GREENE   11/03/2000

54

```
 1   It's spontaneous and instinctive.

 2           He said I don't know.  I don't know

 3   what you want beyond that.  I couldn't answer it

 4   any more specifically.  I don't expect him to.

 5   So don't answer that question again.

 6           MR. ERICKSON:  I want the record

 7   absolutely clear you're instructing your client

 8   not to answer because you think it's been

 9   answered?

10           MR. BERK:  Several times.  Exactly.

11           MR. ERICKSON:  I disagree.  And,

12   Mr. Greene, I suspect we're going to bring you

13   back here for another deposition at some point.

14           MR. BERK:  I suspect we won't.

15           MR. ERICKSON:  I just want you to

16   recognize where the fault lies for that.

17           MR. BERK:  Well, let me make my record.

18           MR. ERICKSON:  Sure.

19           MR. BERK:  He's testified that he did

20   it spontaneously and instinctively.  The

21   follow-up questions were was that accidental or

22   intentional.  The answer to that question is

23   already presumed within the spontaneous and

24   instinctive answer.

25
```

DEPOSITION OBJECTIONS

Depositions (and examinations at trial) aren't meant to be unbounded fishing expeditions. Only certain types of questions can be asked, and a lawyer may object if he or she thinks that the questioning attorney has strayed beyond bounds. Objections both at trial and during depositions generally must be specifically stated and claim more than just that the question is "inadmissible" or "immaterial." In a trial, the judge rules immediately on an objection and will sustain (accept) or overrule (deny) the attorney's objection. In most depositions, however, a judge is not present. As a result, objections are preserved for possible later evaluation. In the meantime, the witness typically still answers the question — unless the witness's attorney is confident that the question is out of bounds, and the answer so sensitive that he or she might instruct the witness not to answer.

Foundation

This objection is raised when the attorney feels that opposing counsel has not provided the proper context for a question. For instance, the question, "Did you hit Mr. Jones with your car?" would not be proper unless it had been established who Mr. Jones was, or that the witness was, in fact, driving on the day in question.

Asked and answered

An attorney raises this objection if he or she feels the witness has already responded to a similar inquiry and further repetition in questioning is being done either to harass the witness or, in the case of a trial, to unfairly repeat answers in front of the jury.

Speculation

An attorney is not allowed to ask a question that calls for the witness to speculate, or guess, as to the answer. The witness should be only asked to answer questions to which he or she has direct knowledge.

Form

An attorney may object not only to a particular question being asked, but also to the manner in which an inquiry is posed. Questions can be objected to for being overly prejudicial (*e.g.*, "Did you negligently clobber Mr. Jones?"), misstating or incompletely stating the prior testimony on which the question is based, or simply being confusing or offering a false premise or choice (*e.g.*, "For how long have you been neglecting your children, six or twelve months?").

Join

An attorney for a co-party can "second" an objection, rather than stating it independently, simply by saying, "Join." Counsel for each party must independently join an objection in order to later raise it respectively in front of a judge.

As you can see from the deposition excerpt, a single moment in time can be examined and re-examined by the lawyers. Joe's deposition turned to other topics after his lawyer objected to continued questioning about "intentional versus accidental," but the issue came up again. Here's part two; you might consider whether Mark's lawyer elicited anything further from Joe on the issue the second time around.

CHARLES E. GREENE   11/03/2000

62

```
 1

 2

 3          THE WITNESS:  You know, I just

 4   reacted.  Probably the only time I even felt any

 5   sense of -- I -- I don't -- I don't think I

 6   ever got angry but when it was over.  I'm saying

 7   that because it happened, it happened so quick.

 8   It happened so quick.

 9          There was no time to be angry because

10   it wasn't precipitated by anger.  It wasn't

11   preplanned.  It was just, as I said, something

12   happened that shouldn't have happened.

13          MR. ERICKSON:  Let's take about a

14   five-minute break, and then I'll finish up.

15          MR. BERK:  Okay.

16          (A recess ensued from 4:04 p.m. until

17   4:13 p.m.)

18          Q.  (BY MR. ERICKSON)  I'd like to talk

19   just a little bit more about this notion that

20   your act of hitting Mr. Cockriel was spontaneous,

21   as you phrased it.

22           Is it your belief that you could not

23   have avoided hitting Mr. Cockriel under the

24   circumstances?

25          A.  Oh, yeah, probably.  Had he not run
```

CHARLES E. GREENE   11/03/2000

63

1 over my foot, it wouldn't even have been in my

2 subconscious, nowhere near.

3   Q. Once he ran over your foot, did you not

4 have any control over whether you hit him or

5 not?

6   A. Oh, I don't want to say I'm that weak,

7 but it was spontaneous. And a spontaneous

8 reaction, meaning it was voluntary, involuntary,

9 you know, what is it? It was a spontaneous

10 reaction. Do you think about it? Spontaneous,

11 probably, probably not.

12   Q. Probably not. I'm sorry. Probably you

13 did not have any control, or probably you did not

14 think about?

15   A. I did not think about it.

16   Q. But you're not saying that you didn't

17 have any control over it, right?

18   A. I don't know if I could say that one

19 way or the other. I mean, no one likes to say

20 that they're helpless, and that's -- that's --

21 that's what you're alluding to. I don't want to

22 say I'm not -- I'm helpless, but it was

23 spontaneous. I don't know how else to say it.

24

25

QUESTIONS

1. Why did Mark's attorney ask Joe so many questions about Joe's position relative to the cart?
2. Why did Mark's attorney continually ask Joe about his mindset right before he hit Mark? Why did Joe's answers not satisfy him?
3. In your opinion, did Joe answer the attorney's questions completely?
4. Can you think of any additional questions Mark's attorney could have asked to elicit a more favorable response from Joe?
5. Aside from the intentional versus accidental line of questioning and corresponding responses, did anything else come up in the deposition that could be of significance to the case?

After Joe's deposition, Joe's lawyers deposed Mark. In the first excerpt reproduced below, Mark describes what he remembers about the incident. (You might consider how it differs from the hypothetical telling of Mark's tale that we offered in Chapter 1, based on the pleadings.)

1

2

3

4

5   Q.   I assume, as you are driving onto the

6   field, you're having to adjust your speed and the

7   direction to avoid people walking?

8   MR. ERICKSON: Object to the form.

9   THE WITNESS: Yeah.

10   Q.   BY MR. BERK: Okay. Any reason why you

11   don't wait or, if you're aware, why the stadium

12   doesn't wait for the field to clear before you drive

13   onto it?

14   A.   I have no idea.

15   Q.   Where were you going when you entered

16   the field? What was your destination?

17   A.   To the 50-yard line.

18   Q.   What was going to happen there?

19   A.   That's where the mix position sits for

20   the show.

21   Q.   Where were you on the field when you

22   first saw Mr. Greene?

23   A.   I don't ever remember seeing him.

24   Q.   Okay. What's the first thing you recall

25   about Mr. Greene on the field?

1   A.   Seeing stars.

2   Q.   Okay. So, is it fair to say, then, you

3   have no recollection of being stopped in your cart

4   near Mr. Greene?

5   A.   I remember being stopped by somebody.

6   Q.   Okay. What do you remember about that?

7   A.   Somebody walked in front of me and I

8   stopped.

9   Q.   Okay. And do you remember any words

10 that were exchanged between you and whoever stopped

11 you?

12   A.   No, I don't.

13   Q.   Would you recognize Mr. Greene if you

14 saw him today?

15   A.   No.

16   Q.   Do you recall anything else about

17 anything that happened on the field before you were

18 struck?

19   A.   Just driving out there.

20   Q.   Okay. Do you recall any verbal exchange

21 with anyone on the field, with the person you were

22 taking in the trailer, with anybody else on the

23 field, any discussion you had with anyone on the

24 field?

25   A.   I don't remember.

1   Q.   Okay.   I assume, then, you don't know,

2   you have no recollection of whether you ran over

3   Mr. Greene's foot?

·4   A.   I don't think so.

.5   Q.   But when you say you don't think so, why

6   don't you think so?

7   A.   Because you can't see.

8   Q.   I don't know what you mean.

9   A.   You can't see the side of the tires.

10   Q.   Okay.   But if I understand your

11   testimony, and maybe I've misunderstood, you have no

12   recollection of what immediately preceded the blow;

13   correct?

14   A.   No.

15   Q.   Is my statement correct?   Just so the

16   record is clear.

17   A.   Yes.

18   Q.   As we sit here today, you don't recall

19   specifically whether you ran over his foot or not?

20   A.   No.

21   Q.   And I'm not going to go through this in

22   great detail.   Nothing else you remember about being

23   struck?   I'll talk to you in a minute about what

24   happened afterwards.   Nothing else you remember about

25   what led up to Mr. Greene striking you or about the

1   actual contact itself?

2   A.   No.

3   Q.   Do you remember where you were hit? And

4   let me separate here. Not from the pain you felt

5   afterwards, but from the actual physical contact.

6   A.   Yes.

7   Q.   Where were you hit?

8   A.   Left side of the face.

9   Q.   Okay. The neck, ear, where

10 specifically?

11   A.   Cheek and the ear.

12   Q.   Cheek and ear?

13   A.   (No oral response.)

14   Q.   Do you know if you were hit with an open

15 hand or a closed hand?

16   A.   I have no idea.

17   Q.   Did you lose consciousness?

18   A.   I don't think so.

19   Q.   Did you fall out of the cart?

20   A.   No.

21   Q.   My understanding is that the blow

22 knocked your glasses off; is that correct?

23   A.   Yes, it did.

24   Q.   Do you remember your glasses getting

25 knocked off or do you just remember going to get them

```
 1  later?

 2          A.   I remember trying to find them --

 3          Q.   Okay.

 4          A.   -- on the cart.

 5          Q.   Okay.  Did you go get them yourself?

 6          A.   No.

 7          Q.   Who got them?

 8          A.   The sound engineer for the band.

 9          Q.   And did you see them on the ground

10  before he picked them up?

11          A.   No.

12          Q.   Do you know how far he went to get them?

13          A.   He said the goalpost.

14          Q.   How far away was that?

15          A.   I was on the 20-yard line, off to the

16  side.

17          Q.   So, 20 yards?  Actually, the goalpost

18  is, I think, at the back of the end zone.  That would

19  be 30 yards.

20          A.   I guess.

21          Q.   Did you watch him walk to get them?

22          A.   No, I did not.

23          Q.   I understand you don't recall what

24  immediately preceded the contact and then maybe even

25  the contact itself.  What is the first thing you do
```

```
 1  recall after being struck?

 2         A.  Driving on over.

 3         Q.  Okay.  Driving over to where?

 4         A.  To where the mix position was going to

 5  sit.

 6         Q.  Describe for me, talking immediately

 7  after the blow and the time you reached mid-field,

 8  tell me what you're feeling physically.

 9         A.  I had no idea what happened.

10         Q.  Okay.

11         A.  I couldn't hear.  My ears were ringing.

12  I had no idea what happened.

13         Q.  Okay.  After you were struck, did you

14  stay at the point of the striking for any length of

15  time or did you immediately get your glasses back and

16  drive to the center?

17         A.  No, I stayed there for what seemed like

18  a few minutes.

19         Q.  Okay.  So, you didn't know what

20  happened.  When you reached mid-field, were your ears

21  ringing?

22         A.  Yes.

23         Q.  Did you have pain?

24         A.  Yes.

25         Q.  And that would be where?
```

MARK COCKRIEL - 1/8/01   29

```
 1          A.  On the side of my head and my ears.
 2          Q.  Okay.  Did you have a headache?
 3          A.  Shortly after.
 4          Q.  Okay.  Were you bleeding anywhere?
 5          A.  No.
 6          Q.  Did you then proceed to do whatever you
 7   needed to do to set up the sound at mid-field?
 8          A.  Yes.
 9          Q.  How long did that process take?
10          A.  I don't know.
11          Q.  I think you told me earlier, is that in
12   the 15-minute range, generally?
13          A.  Yes.
14          Q.  Up until the time you finished setting
15   up the sound, did you talk to anyone about the
16   incident?
17          A.  No.
18          Q.  Did anyone, up to that point in time,
19   administer first-aid to you or ask you if you were
20   okay, anything like that?
21          A.  No.
22          Q.  Did the person in the back of the truck,
23   Randy, whatever his name was, say anything to you
24   while you were on the field?
25          A.  Yeah, he finally told me who the guy
```

```
 1    was.
 2              Q.   Did he tell you anything else?
 3              A.   No.
 4              Q.   So, you finish setting up the sound,
 5    then what?
 6              A.   Concert started.
 7              Q.   What did you do?
 8              A.   I stood by the mix position, made sure
 9    everything was okay.
10              Q.   Did you stay there the whole concert?
11              A.   No.
12              Q.   How long did you stay there?
13              A.   I don't remember.
14              Q.   Would it typically be that you would
15    stay there the whole, entire concert?
16              A.   Yes.
17              Q.   Why didn't you do that on this occasion?
18              A.   The representatives from the Cardinals
19    came and got me.
20              Q.   Do you recall who specifically came and
21    got you?
22              A.   No, I don't.
23              Q.   What did they tell you when they came to
24    see you?
25              A.   They told me that Greene hit me and
```

```
 1   wanted me to have their doctor look at me.
 2            Q.   And you went with them and saw the team
 3   doctor?
 4            A.   Yes.
 5            Q.   Approximately how long after the blow
 6   did you see the team doctor?
 7            A.   15 minutes.
 8            Q.   At that point, did you have a headache?
 9            A.   I don't remember.
10            Q.   Did you still have ringing in your ears?
11            A.   Yes, I did.
12            Q.   What were your other physical symptoms?
13            A.   Dizzy.
14            Q.   Okay.  Anything else?
15            A.   No.
16            Q.   Still had some pain?
17            A.   Yes.
18            Q.   Any swelling?
19            A.   Starting to swell.
20            Q.   How long did the Cardinals team
21   physician examine you?
22            A.   Five minutes.
23            Q.   What did he do?
24            A.   Looked in my ear and gave me two
25   aspirin.
```

```
1            Q.   Okay.  Did the swelling get worse?

2            A.   Yes.

3            Q.   Okay.  When was it at its worst?

4            A.   The following day.

5            Q.   Did you or your wife or anyone else take

6    a picture of your face to show the swelling?

7            A.   I don't remember if we did or not.

8            Q.   Have you seen a picture of your face at

9    the time?

10           A.   At that time, no.

11           Q.   I mean, since then, have you ever seen a

12   picture of what your face looked like back then?

13           A.   No.

14           Q.   Where specifically was the swelling?

15           A.   Right side of my face, cheek and ear.

16           Q.   After seeing the Cardinals team doctor,

17   did you later see any physicians or audiologists

18   regarding your ears?

19           A.   Yes.

20           Q.   When did you first go to see someone?

21           A.   I don't remember how long afterwards.

22   It was a few weeks afterwards.

23           Q.   And what led you to go to see someone?

24           A.   The ringing didn't stop.

25
```

Joe Greene is a public figure; a famous sports star from the 1970s. Wholly apart from his on-field talent, Joe is also widely known to fans of the time for a nationwide commercial in which he appeared in the early 1980s. It featured Joe in his Pittsburgh Steelers football uniform, dejected after a tough game, and then cheered by a child who gives him his Coke. Joe tosses his jersey to the child ("Hey,

kid — catch!"), who exclaims, "Thanks, Mean Joe!"[2] A *New York Times* article from 1980 described the commercial, and its impact on Joe's reputation as follows:

> [A major reason] for the change in the public perception of Joe Greene was what is normally regarded as a total irrelevancy in pro football — a television commercial. Only this was one of the great commercials of the ages. In it, a worn-and-battered Joe Greene, presumably injured, limps down the tunnel of a football stadium, wearing his shoulder pads, his game-worn jersey slung over his shoulder. A small boy follows, partly in awe, partly in sympathy. Greene is too tired, perhaps too depressed, to exchange civilities with him. The boy offers him the most precious thing he possesses: his bottle of Coke. At first reluctant, Joe finally accepts it, then drinks it down without pausing. The boy turns to go, a faint suggestion of disappointment — over failing to make a human connection — in his slumped shoulders. Joe calls to him. "Hey, kid . . . here!" He throws his jersey to him and endows him with a wonderfully warm, grateful smile. "Wow!" says the boy. "Thanks a million, Joe!"
>
> The commercial was released to the networks on Oct. 1, 1979, and it had an immediate, enormous impact. It was rated first in popularity among consumers interviewed by an independent testing firm, and it won eight national and international awards, including a Clio for Joe Greene as the best male performer in a television commercial.
>
> It also had an immense influence in changing his image. For when he turned around to face the young boy, he was no longer Mean Joe Greene, observed William Van Loan, who was then director of marketing operations for Coca-Cola U.S.A. "He was Othello." People noticed things about him that they'd never quite noticed before. "He looks like he smiles from the middle of his soul," said the wife of a Pittsburgh sports writer.[3]

Joe's attorneys asked questions about Mark's recollection of the incident and how it might relate to the commercial in the following two excerpts from Mark's deposition.

---

[2] The U.S. Library of Congress has archived the ad on the Internet; to view it, go to <http://memory.loc.gov/ammem/ccmphtml/colahome.html>.

[3] William Barry Furlong, "Football Violence," *New York Times* (Nov. 30, 1980), 36. The boy in the ad says "Thanks, Mean Joe!" rather than "Thanks a million," but the article's description is otherwise accurate.

```
 1

 2

 3

 4          Q.   What was your perception of his

 5   reputation based on that commercial?

 6          A.   I don't know.

 7          Q.   Okay.  Angry?

 8          A.   I don't know.

 9          Q.   Mean?

10          A.   (No oral response.)

11          Q.   Don't know?

12          A.   Don't know.

13          Q.   Didn't have one?

14          A.   Didn't have one.

15          Q.   Anything about that commercial that

16   would suggest to you anything about his reputation on

17   or off the field?

18          A.   No.

19          Q.   Did Mr. Greene at all ever taunt you

20   before you restarted your cart and ran over his foot?

21          A.   No.

22          Q.   Did Mr. Greene threaten you before you

23   restarted your cart and ran over his foot?

24          A.   No.

25          Q.   Were you in any way trying to get away
```

 1 from or avoid Mr. Greene as you restarted your cart

 2 and ran over his foot?

 3   MR. ERICKSON: Object to the form.

 4   THE WITNESS: I don't know.

 5   Q. BY MR. KENNEDY: You didn't feel any

 6 sense of "I've got to get away from this guy," did

 7 you?

 8   A. No.

 9   Q. Have you made any claim for workers'

10 compensation for your injuries?

11   A. No.

12   Q. You were injured on the job; right?

13   A. Yes.

14   Q. Is there any reason you haven't made a

15 workers' compensation claim?

16   A. No.

17   Q. I think you told me about the season of

18 1998 that you were on the field for a half time

19 production. I believe, and I could be wrong, you

20 also told me that there was another occasion that you

21 were on the field at Sun Devil Stadium before October

22 of 1999; is that right?

23   A. Yes.

24   Q. When was the other occasion?

25   A. I don't remember, a football game.

```
 1                    RE-EXAMINATION
 2   BY MR. BERK:
 3          Q.  Mr. Cockriel, as you watched the video,
 4   does it appear to you that after your cart is
 5   stopped, it started up again before you were slapped?
 6          A.  I don't remember.
 7          Q.  Okay.  That's all I have.
 8              MR. ERICKSON:  Read and sign.
 9              (The deposition was concluded at
10   10:51 a.m.)
11
12
13
14              _____
                                MARK COCKRIEL
15
16
17
18
19
20
21
22
23
24
25
```

QUESTIONS

1. How would you compare Mark's and Joe's credibility as witnesses?

2. After reading the depositions, is the assault and battery case against Joe more or less clear than you previously believed it to be — or unchanged?

3. If you had been Joe's lawyer, what would you have viewed as the most important response to elicit from Mark in the deposition? Was that response elicited in the testimony reproduced above?

4. If you were Joe's lawyer, are there any additional questions that you would have asked Mark?

WRITTEN EXERCISE

After the depositions of Mark and Joe, the attorney provisionally assigned for Joe by the Cardinals' insurance company prepared a memorandum for Joe and the company, describing the progress of the case and summarizing the depositions.

Draft your own brief memo summarizing the two previous depositions. Be sure to include the relevant facts from each witness, and how those facts relate to the case at hand. See the introduction to such a memo, including a summary of the procedural process, that follows.

Re: Claim #   :
         Insured   :   Charles Edward Greene and Agnes Greene
         Claimant :   Mark Cockriel
         D/Loss   :   10/31/99

Dear Mr. Watkins:

The purpose of this letter is to update the status of this matter and to provide you with a supplemental evaluation.

PROCEDURAL STATUS

This case has not yet been set for trial. Within the last week, however, Plaintiff filed a motion asking the Court to schedule a trial date for on or after July 2, 2001. Our best guess is that trial will be scheduled for sometime in August or September of this year.

DISCOVERY

Discovery is largely complete. The only person we have deposed to date is the Plaintiff, Mark Cockriel, and the only other person we are certain we want to depose is Randy Piotroski. Mr. Piotroski witnessed the incident, and based upon our telephonic interview of him, we think it is important to schedule his deposition. Hopefully, we will complete that deposition within the next month.

APR 02 '01 11:18AM   P.3/13

JONES, SKELTON & HOCHULI, P.L.C.
ATTORNEYS AT LAW

March 27, 2001
Page 2
_____

We also may need to depose three medical providers recently disclosed by Plaintiff. Specifically, in a recent Disclosure Statement (enclosed), Plaintiff identified Dr. Mark Baldree, Dr. Charles Meinstin, and audiologist Bonnie Quinn as expert witnesses who will testify about Mr. Cockriel's injuries, his prognosis and the long-term risks associated with injuries such as the one he suffered. We are still in the process of reviewing medical records to determine whether it is necessary to depose these medical providers, and should we decide that one or more depositions are appropriate, we will request authority.

In terms of Plaintiff's discovery, Plaintiff has already deposed our client (your insured), Mr. Greene, and has scheduled the depositions of Michael Bidwell, the President of the Arizona Cardinals, and David McGinnis, the Cardinals' head coach. Both depositions are scheduled for April 16, 2001, but we anticipate that the Arizona Cardinals will seek a protective order.

Recall that Mark's deposition referenced the presence of a sound engineer in the trailer attached to the sound cart. That makes him a natural witness to the incident; excerpts from his deposition by Joe's lawyer are reprinted below.

DEPOSITION OF RANDALL ROBERT PIOTROSKI - 6/28/01

44

```
 1

 2

 3      Q.   Do you recall that there was no one in the

 4  immediate vicinity around Mr. Greene?

 5      A.   No.   There were people around Mr. Greene.   Not

 6  like right next to him like we are here, but there was

 7  plenty of people within 5 feet of him.

 8      Q.   I think you started to tell me that right about

 9  the time that Mr. Cockriel stopped the cart Mr. Greene

10  said something?

11      A.   That's at the point that Mr. Greene said, "You

12  are aware there are people out here on this field?"

13              And Mark's answer to him, very nicely, "Yes,

14  sir, I do."  I do mean "Yes, sir."  That is what he said.

15      Q.   And what did Mr. Greene say?

16      A.   He said, "Well, you will need to be a little more

17  careful.  You could have run me over."

18      Q.   And then what happened?

19      A.   And Mark said, "I'm trying to be as careful as I

20  can be.  I have no intentions of running anyone over."

21  And Mr. Greene was more or less, the inflection in his

22  voice is, well, you are being a smart ass.  It was kind of

23  the attitude or air that he came back to us with.

24      Q.   Well be candid.  Was Mr. Cockriel being syrupy

25  sweet with his responses?
```

DEPOSITION OF RANDALL ROBERT PIOTROSKI - 6/28/01

45

```
 1        A.    No.   He was being a respectful individual, the
 2   same way I would be.
 3        Q.    And then what happened after Mr. Cockriel said,
 4   "I'm not trying to run anyone over"?
 5               MR. ERICKSON:  Object to the form.
 6               THE WITNESS:  Say it again.
 7   BY MR. BERK:
 8        Q.    I think you described for me a conversation that
 9   took place --
10        A.    Right.
11        Q.    -- or exchange of comments by Mr. Greene and
12   responses by Mr. Cockriel, and I -- let's confirm what the
13   last piece of that conversation was.
14               I think you told me that Mr. Cockriel
15   politely said that he was --
16        A.    He was not going to hit anyone or he was trying
17   to avoid anyone.
18        Q.    And during this, at that point in the
19   conversation, are they still about 6 feet apart?
20        A.    No.
21               MR. ERICKSON:  Object; form.
22   BY MR. BERK:
23        Q.    How had they gotten closer?
24        A.    Well, I mean, they haven't changed from the
25   position that they stopped and started to talk at.
```

DEPOSITION OF RANDALL ROBERT PIOTROSKI - 6/28/01
                                                              46

```
 1       Q.    Which was a couple of feet?
 2       A.    Mr. Greene is at the very nose of this tractor,
 3   which is a riding lawn mower basically, and Mr. Cockriel
 4   is sitting in the seat, so maybe 2 feet between them, and
 5   this conversation ensues.
 6       Q.    How far away from Mr. Greene in terms of feet
 7   were you at that point?
 8       A.    I would say a maximum of 6 feet.
 9       Q.    What happened after the last part of the
10   conversation?
11       A.    Mr. Greene said, "You need to make sure you are
12   being careful."
13             Mark says, "Yes, sir.  I am doing that.  I'm
14   trying to take my time," is what Mark said.
15             And Mr. Greene said, "Well, just see that
16   you be careful and watch out for people."
17             And at that same time as he is saying that
18   to Mark, out of my peripheral vision is when I see
19   Mr. Greene's foot sliding towards the front tire of the
20   truck.
21       Q.    Which front tire?  As you are sitting in the
22   driver's seat the right or left front?
23       A.    His back is to that camera, if I am not mistaken
24   in the videotape, so it would be the right front tire.
25       Q.    Effectively the passenger?
```

DEPOSITION OF RANDALL ROBERT PIOTROSKI - 6/28/01

```
 1        A.    Passenger front wheel.

 2        Q.    And as you were sitting in the trailer, were you

 3   in the middle of the trailer?

 4        A.    More towards the front end of the trailer, not in

 5   exactly the middle.

 6        Q.    Toward the front end, but from the left to right

 7   perspective, I assume you were generally centered?

 8        A.    Yes.

 9        Q.    And explain to me what you saw Mr. Greene do.

10        A.    At the same moment as they are talking, I see his

11   foot slide across the lawn.  And it only had to slight

12   about 7 or 8 inches.  He was standing kind of like this

13   (indicating).  My feet are in an L, okay?

14              As he was talking, his foot moved like this

15   (indicating) to where his feet were parallel to each

16   other.  And at that point, that puts the tractor, the

17   wheel of the tractor between his two feet.  He has one

18   foot on one side of the wheel, and one foot on the other

19   side of the wheel and proceeds to tell Mark to drive on

20   through, just go ahead and drive through.

21        Q.    Do you have some reason to believe when

22   Mr. Greene repositioned his feet or foot he was doing so

23   to impede the wheel as opposed to just repositioning his

24   feet or moving his body?

25        A.    I don't know that he was trying to impede the
```

```
 1  | wheel.
 2  |     Q.    Okay.  But for whatever reason his feet moved?
 3  |     A.    Yes.
 4  |     Q.    Okay.  And was there some reason why Mr. Cockriel
 5  | wouldn't have been able to observe what you observed in
 6  | terms of his repositioning?
 7  |     A.    Yes.  Because Mr. Cockriel is sitting in the
 8  | tractor; there's a fender skirt here, motor in front of
 9  | him, and he is making direct eye-to-eye contact with
10  | Mr. Greene.  His eyes never moved.
11  |     Q.    If Mr. Greene is close enough to the cart to have
12  | his foot in front of the wheel, I assume he is within a
13  | foot of the cart; is that fair?
14  |     A.    Yes.
15  |     Q.    And Mr. Greene said, "Drive on," or did he say
16  | something beyond that?
17  |     A.    He said, "Drive on and be careful about it."
18  | Those were his words.
19  |     Q.    Did Mr. Cockriel respond by saying --
20  |     A.    Mark said, "Yes, sir."
21  |     Q.    And he didn't say, "No.  You go first"?
22  |     A.    No, he didn't.
23  |     Q.    And in response to Mr. Greene's statement, did
24  | Mr. Cockriel start?
25  |     A.    He said, "Yes, sir.  I'll move on," and he moved
```

DEPOSITION OF RANDALL ROBERT PIOTROSKI - 6/28/01

49

```
 1   forward.  And instantly the cart goes up and down, and
 2   this big arm comes flying into everybody's vision and hits
 3   Mark.
 4        Q.   I assume then it was probably a second or so
 5   between the time, maybe less than a second between the
 6   time Mr. Cockriel started the cart and the time it ran
 7   over Mr. Greene's foot?
 8        A.   Say that again.
 9        Q.   I assume that it must have been no more than a
10   second or two between the time that Mr. Cockriel started
11   forward and the time the wheel of the cart ran over Mr.
12   Greene's foot?
13             MR. ERICKSON:  Objection; form.
14   BY MR. BERK:
15        Q.   If I understand your testimony, Mr. Greene's foot
16   was right next to the wheel?
17        A.   Yes.
18        Q.   So basically as soon as Mr. Cockriel started
19   forward --
20        A.   He went over his foot, yes.
21        Q.   And if I understood what you were saying a minute
22   ago, basically as soon as it went over his foot --
23        A.   He hit him.
24        Q.   -- Mr. Greene's big arm came across and hit him?
25        A.   Yes.
```

DEPOSITION OF RANDALL ROBERT PIOTROSKI - 6/28/01

50

1   Q.   And less than a second maybe in between?

2   A.   Yes.

3   Q.   Did Mr. Greene say anything after he hit him?

4   A.   I believe he said, "I told you you were going to

5   hurt someone."

6   Q.   And that would have been after he struck him in

7   the face?

8   A.   Yes.

9   Q.   And I want to get into the actual impact in a

10   minute.

11   But did Mr. Cockriel say anything in

12   response?

13   A.   No.

14   Q.   Did you say anything in response or at that point

15   after?

16   A.   No. I was shocked. I was just like --

17   Q.   Did anybody else in the vicinity say anything

18   that you heard after the blow?

19   A.   No, sir.

QUESTIONS

1. Did you notice any differences between the facts as told by the sound engineer in the above deposition and the facts given by Joe and Mark in their depositions?

2. Do you think this deposition went well or poorly for Joe's attorney? Are there any aspects of the testimony that are especially likely either to help or to hurt Mark's case?

3. If you completed the written exercise above, what, if any, changes would you make to the memo you wrote based on this deposition?

4. After this deposition, should any of the parties' case strategies change in any way?

After the deposition of Randy, Joe's attorney prepared another memorandum. The memorandum describes Randy's testimony in terms of the significance it has to the theory of the case Joe's attorney might plan to assert at trial.

COPY

JS&H | JONES, SKELTON & HOCHULI, P.L.C.

Re: Claim #   :
      Insured   :   Charles Edward Greene and Agnes Greene
      Claimant   :   Mark Cockriel
      D/Loss   :   10/31/99

Dear Mr. Watkins:

On June 28, 2001, we deposed Randy Piotroski, a witness to the incident in question. With your authorization, we shared with our co-defendant, the Arizona Cardinals, the cost of bringing Mr. Piotroski to Phoenix for the deposition. The following is a summary of his testimony.

DEPOSITION OBJECTIVES

As you may recall from a prior report, when we interviewed Mr. Piotroski several months ago, he said three things which caused us concern. First, he said that Mr. Greene precipitated the confrontation by walking in front of the cart driven by Plaintiff. Second, he told us that while Mr. Cockriel and Mr. Greene were talking prior to the point at which Mr. Greene struck Mr. Cockriel, Mr. Greene "intentionally" slid his foot in front of the vehicle's tire, and that after doing so, Mr. Greene instructed Plaintiff to "drive on". During the interview, Mr. Piotroski told us that although he saw Mr. Greene move his foot, Plaintiff, who had a different vantage point, could not. Third, Mr. Piotroski told us that after Mr. Cockriel ran over Mr. Greene's foot, but before Mr. Greene struck Mr. Cockriel, Mr. Greene said something like, "I told you you were going to hit someone". Mr. Piotroski's recollection in this regard was inconsistent with our position that Mr. Greene struck Plaintiff as an instinctive reaction to being run over, and consistent with Plaintiff's allegation that Mr. Greene acted with premeditation.

CREDIBILITY/DEMEANOR

Mr. Piotroski is middle-aged, mild-mannered, and, in our opinion, very credible. As a result, we believe he will make an above-average witness at trial.

JONES, SKELTON & HOCHULI, P.L.C.

July 23, 2001
Page 2 _____

SUMMARY OF TESTIMONY

Mr. Piotroski testified that he travels with various rock and roll bands and serves as a sound technician. In layman's terms, he is a "roadie" who sets up the stage, microphones and speakers prior to rock concerts. His primary employer is Carlos Santana, although he has toured with several bands. On the date in question, he was working for a band called Big Bad Voodoo Daddy.

Although we suspected that Plaintiff and Mr. Piotroski might have been friends, or that they at least had some social relationship, Mr. Piotroski testified that he has never met or spoken to Plaintiff other than on the day in question. On that date, Plaintiff and Mr. Piotroski worked together to do the sound set-up for a post-game concert at Sun Devil Stadium. Mr. Piotroski testified that he and Plaintiff exchanged pleasantries while they worked, but that the conversation was very light.

Mr. Piotroski told us that some of the sound equipment was in a trailer behind a cart, and that when the game ended, Plaintiff drove the cart onto the field. Mr. Piotroski rode in the trailer so he could make sure the sound equipment did not fall off. Mr. Piotroski said that both he and the Plaintiff were looking straight ahead, and that their objective was to get on the field as soon as possible to prepare for the concert.

Mr. Piotroski did not remember how much pedestrian traffic was on the field when the game ended, but he recalled that Plaintiff stopped the cart at least once to avoid pedestrians. Mr. Piotroski acknowledged that Plaintiff could have waited until all pedestrian traffic cleared before entering the field, or could have taken a different route which would have avoided all pedestrian traffic. Mr. Piotroski further acknowledged that although these alternatives might have taken longer, the additional time would not have been a significant factor.

According to Mr. Piotroski, he saw Mr. Greene from approximately ten yards away. He said that Mr. Greene had a "pained" and "angry" look on his face, but he did not recall whether Mr. Greene was looking down or up. Mr. Piotroski testified that Mr. Greene and the cart were on a course to intersect, and that if neither had stopped, there would have been a collision. Mr. Piotroski testified that the cart and Mr. Greene stopped a few feet from each other, and then Mr. Greene proceeded to lecture Plaintiff about safe driving. Mr. Piotroski could not recall all the details of that conversation, but he did recall that Mr. Greene warned Plaintiff that Plaintiff had to be more careful, and that if he was not more careful, he was likely to hit someone. According to Mr. Piotroski, Plaintiff politely accepted the lecture and told Mr. Greene that he was doing, and would continue to do, the best that he could.

Jones, Skelton & Hochuli, P.L.C.

According to Mr. Piotroski, while Plaintiff and Mr. Greene were having the above-described conversation, Mr. Greene repositioned his foot so that it was in front of the cart's front tire. Mr. Piotroski further explained that although he could see, from his vantage point in the trailer, that Mr. Greene moved his foot in front of the tire, Plaintiff, from his vantage point, could not. As a result, according to Mr. Piotroski, when Mr. Greene finished his lecture and instructed Plaintiff to "drive on", Plaintiff had no way of knowing that he would run over Mr. Greene's foot.

Because Mr. Piotroski was effectively accusing Mr. Greene of intentionally getting Plaintiff to run over his foot, we asked Mr. Piotroski several follow-up questions, and we believe we significantly limited the impact of his testimony. First, Mr. Piotroski admitted that he did not know if Mr. Greene intentionally placed his foot in front of the cart so that it would be run over, and acknowledged that Mr. Greene simply may have been repositioning his feet so that he could face Plaintiff while they were talking. Second, while Mr. Piotroski maintained that he saw Mr. Greene move his foot and that Plaintiff did not, Mr. Piotroski's testimony in this regard was very shaky. Simply stated, given the location of the people involved, we do not think a jury will believe that Mr. Piotroski, who was obviously much farther away from Mr. Greene than was Plaintiff, had a unique vantage point where he could see what Plaintiff could not. Finally, and most importantly, when we watched the videotape of the incident with Mr. Piotroski, he admitted that based upon his review of the videotape, it does not appear that Mr. Greene moved his foot at all, and Mr. Piotroski was unable to explain the discrepancy between his recollection and the videotape.

Mr. Piotroski testified that when Mr. Greene instructed Plaintiff to "drive on", Mr. Cockriel slowly moved the cart forward and ran over Mr. Greene's foot. Mr. Piotroski said that there was no question in his mind but that the cart ran over Mr. Greene's foot, and that he saw that corner of the cart go up and down as if it had gone over a bump. Although Mr. Piotroski told us, during our interview several months ago, that Mr. Greene said something (i.e., "I told you you were going to run over someone") after Plaintiff ran over his foot but before Mr. Greene hit Plaintiff, his deposition testimony was otherwise. Specifically, Mr. Piotroski testified at his deposition that Mr. Greene struck Plaintiff immediately after being run over, and that Mr. Greene did not say anything in between. Mr. Piotroski's testimony in this regard was obviously very important because it undermines Plaintiff's claim that Mr. Greene acted with premeditation, and it supports our argument that Mr. Greene's slap was an instinctive response to being run over.

Mr. Piotroski testified that Mr. Greene's slap knocked Plaintiff's glasses thirty feet through the air. Upon further examination, however, Mr. Piotroski admitted that he never saw the glasses land, and that the only basis for his conclusion that they flew thirty feet was because the incident occurred at about the 10-yard line and someone later found the eyeglasses in the end zone. Mr. Piotroski admitted that he has no way of knowing whether the glasses flew into the end zone or whether they got there by some other means (e.g., they were inadvertently kicked there by pedestrian traffic or intentionally moved by someone). In any event, Mr. Piotroski testified that Plaintiff drove

JONES, SKELTON & HOCHULI, P.L.C.

July 23, 2001
Page 4

the cart to the set-up point at the middle of the field, and that Plaintiff, Mr. Piotroski and the other sound people then completed the pre-game set-up.

According to Mr. Piotroski, Plaintiff had a welt on his cheek and ear where he had been struck, and Plaintiff complained of dizziness and a ringing in his ears. Mr. Piotroski admitted, however, that Plaintiff appeared to be able to complete his job function without limitation.

During the last portion of Mr. Piotroski's deposition, the attorney representing the Arizona Cardinals asked Mr. Piotroski several questions about conversations Mr. Piotroski allegedly had with representatives from the Cardinals' organization. Specifically, in an Affidavit Mr. Piotroski previously submitted in connection with this case, Mr. Piotroski stated that shortly after the incident, two representatives from the Cardinals told him that there were previous instances of inappropriate behavior by Mr. Greene, and that the Cardinals were "tired of it". At his deposition, however, Mr. Piotroski backed away from his testimony somewhat. Specifically, he admitted that he was not sure that the people talking were employed by the Cardinals, and he could not recall in detail what they said. The significance of Mr. Piotroski's testimony in this regard is that one of Plaintiff's claims in this case is that the Cardinals had prior, negative experiences with Mr. Greene, that they should have terminated him as a result of those experiences, and that by not doing so, they negligently caused Plaintiff's injuries.

SIGNIFICANCE OF TESTIMONY

Mr. Piotroski's testimony was important in several respects. First, he confirmed that there were options available to Plaintiff which would have minimized, if not eliminated, the possibility of a confrontation. Specifically, he acknowledged that Plaintiff could have waited until all pedestrian traffic cleared, or could have taken a route onto the field which would not have crossed paths with any pedestrians.

Second, Mr. Piotroski admitted that based upon the videotape, it does not appear that Mr. Greene moved his foot in front of the cart, and that even if Mr. Greene did move his foot, he may have done so inadvertently as he was talking to Plaintiff.

Third, Mr. Piotroski recanted his earlier statement to us that Mr. Greene said something to Plaintiff after Plaintiff ran over Mr. Greene's foot but before Mr. Greene struck Plaintiff, and testified that Mr. Greene struck Plaintiff immediately after being run over. As stated above, this was probably the most significant aspect of Mr. Piotroski's deposition in that it significantly undermines Plaintiff's claim that Mr. Greene hit Plaintiff with premeditation and that Mr. Greene should be assessed punitive damages as a result.

JONES, SKELTON & HOCHULI, P.L.C.

July 23, 2001
Page 5

       This case remains set for trial on December 4, 2001, although we recently filed a motion to postpone the trial until after the regular season ends. If you have any questions about Mr. Piotroski's deposition, or about any other aspect of this case, please feel free to call.

Very truly yours,

WRITTEN EXERCISE

Based on the depositions above, create two statements of facts: one meant to persuade the trier of fact of Joe's position, and another meant to persuade the trier of fact of Mark's position. You may find the charts that follow to be helpful.

CHART A: ASSAULT AND BATTERY[2]

Element	Relevant Doctrinal Nuances[3]	Relevant Factual Questions	Relevant Facts
Assault			
Act (by the defendant)	An act requires an exercise of will or volition, and cannot be a mere reflex (such as kicking out when a doctor hits your knee).[4]	Was Joe's arm movement a reflexive response or an "act"?	
Intent to cause harmful or offensive contact or an imminent apprehension of such contact	Even if the defendant's purpose is not to cause harm, if the defendant acts with the knowledge that, to a substantial certainty, imminent apprehension of harmful or offensive contact will result, he "intends" the contact.[5]	Did Joe intend either harmful contact or for Mark to experience "imminent apprehension" of such contact?	
Imminent apprehension of offensive contact actually results		Did Mark have an "imminent apprehension" that Joe would strike him?	

[2] At this stage of the analysis, we consider only the prima facie elements of the case. The defendant can win either by arguing that the plaintiff has failed to prove the prima facie case or by arguing that an applicable defense or privilege bars liability.

[3] Of course, the doctrinal nuances in this chart are not an exhaustive list of the doctrinal nuances important to these claims. These are merely the nuances most important to this case. In other words, don't rely on this chart as an exhaustive way to prepare for the assault and battery portion of, say, a torts exam.

[4] See Restatement (Second) of Torts § 2 cmt. b (1965).

[5] See Restatement (Second) of Torts § 21 cmt. d (1965).

CHART A: ASSAULT AND BATTERY[2] (*Continued*)

Element	Relevant Doctrinal Nuances[3]	Relevant Factual Questions	Relevant Facts
Battery			
Act (by the defendant)	An act requires an exercise of will or volition, and cannot be a mere reflex (such as kicking out when a doctor hits your knee).[6]	Was Joe's striking Mark a reflexive response or an "act"?	
Intent to cause harmful or offensive contact	Intent to cause the *harm* sustained by the plaintiff is NOT required for liability. Intent to cause the *contact* is sufficient.	Did Joe intend to cause contact with Mark?	
Harmful contact results	For liability to be imposed, it is NOT necessary that the harm that actually results is the same as the harm intended by the defendant.	Was Mark harmed by the contact?	

[6] See Restatement (Second) of Torts § 2 cmt. b (1965).

At this point, you may or may not be convinced that the initially clear-seeming claim against Joe has become complicated by greater scrutiny of the facts. Suppose (contrary to the pleadings in the real case) that Joe brought a counterclaim against Mark for running over his foot with the cart. Would that act constitute a clear case of assault and battery?

3

THE MURKY LINE BETWEEN INTENTIONAL TORTS AND NEGLIGENCE

> **THE BASICS**
>
> **Negligence:** It is often convenient to analyze negligence using the following five elements:
>
> - **Duty** — The plaintiff had some right that the defendant had a duty to avoid infringing.
>
> - **Breach** — The defendant's act or failure to act constitutes a breach of this duty.
>
> - **Proximate Cause** — The defendant's conduct is close enough in the causal chain to the harm felt by plaintiff as to be a proximate cause of the harm.
>
> - **Cause in Fact** — The harm would not have occurred but for the defendant's conduct.
>
> - **Harm** — The plaintiff experienced some compensable damage as a result of the defendant's conduct.

If you have worked through Chapter 1 and reviewed the basics of assault and battery at the beginning of Chapter 2, you may be wondering why you are preparing to read about negligence in a case that seems like an obvious case of intentional tort. There are several answers, many of which are related to which parties or firms in addition to Joe might turn out to be legally responsible for any liabilities. For example, for reasons that are explored in Chapter 5 on insurance issues, the *plaintiff* may want to be able to establish that the incident was not an intentional tort, or at least not entirely intentional. Insurance policies covering tortious liability are common, but they often only cover cases of negligence, not intentional tort. Thus, if an insured defendant were to be personally insolvent (or simply poor), the plaintiff could still collect from the defendant's insurance policy.

Further, the Arizona Cardinals, Joe's employer, is likely to have much deeper pockets than Joe himself and is far less likely to be judgment proof. As a result, it is in the plaintiff's interests to try to characterize the team as liable, either through vicarious liability or independent negligence. If Joe's acts can be characterized as negligent, the Cardinals may be more likely to be vicariously liable for Joe's actions. Moreover, the Cardinals may be liable on an independent theory of negligence directly attributable to the team — negligent hiring or negligent supervision.

In the real case, Mark's initial complaint included assault and battery, but did not include a negligence claim against Joe. However, Mark did not have to choose between alleging that Joe was liable for assault and battery and alleging that Joe was liable for negligence. Mark could have (and in a later amended complaint did) put both causes of action in the same complaint, by *pleading in the alternative.* Pleading in the alternative allows the plaintiff to allege both causes of action at once, even though the causes of action might be based on contradicting interpretations of the facts and/or law.

Pleading in the alternative can become strategically difficult as lawyers need to develop a theory of the case that can be argued persuasively to a jury. When contradictory arguments must be made to support alternative theories, it becomes increasingly difficult to give a coherent description of the facts that supports both theories. Moreover, the decision about which theory of the case to pursue can affect the way in which questions are asked at depositions. Had Mark pled in the alternative, his lawyer may have found it difficult to develop the facts necessary to support an assault and battery claim without seriously impairing the negligence claim. On the other hand, pleading different causes of action in the early stages of a case preserves options at trial no matter which direction the factual development takes.

As is apparent from the depositions and strategy memoranda included in Chapter 2, the most contested issue on the assault and battery claim is the issue of whether Joe *intended* to hit Mark. Joe's assertion seems to be that his swat was reflexive, that there was no opportunity to think and therefore, no time to form an intention of any kind. If indeed Joe's act was purely reflexive — like the kick induced by a rubber mallet to the knee — then Joe has no liability for an intentional tort nor, without some claim of hyper-reflexive tendencies, liability in negligence, either. A spontaneous, reflexive reaction is merely an unfortunate accident, unless the defendant had advance reason to think that he was particularly susceptible to sudden, uncontrollable outbursts. For instance, if a person knew that she suffered fainting spells at least once a day, it could well be negligent for her to drive a car if the condition could not be controlled.

Where, then, between an intentional slap and a reflexive (and therefore innocent) one, could negligence fit in?

Perhaps one could claim that a person who indeed intentionally hurts someone also fails to exercise a reasonable standard of care as to the other person's safety. Without the strategic issues involving vicarious liability or insurance in the mix, this claim need never be doctrinally tested — one could simply allege battery and leave out any "lesser included offense" of negligence, especially since intentional torts open the door to an award of punitive damages. But the aforementioned strategic issues *are* in the mix, and have compelled courts to address the issue.

For example, in the following case, the plaintiff was knocked unconscious by the defendant after being asked to "step outside," and yet sued only for negligence, apparently so as to be able to trigger coverage from the defendant's insurance policy. Here the defendant and his insurance company-appointed lawyers argue that his actions *were* intentional — to spare the insurance company a negligence verdict — and also in self-defense, to shield the defendant from an independent claim of battery, on which he would be personally liable. The plaintiff argues that the defendant's punch was not intentional, eliciting testimony about the punch being a "reflexive" reaction, strikingly similar to the exchanges in the deposition excerpts in Chapter 2. Thus, the arguments in the following excerpt seem quite similar to those in the case of Mark against Joe — except for the fact that the plaintiff and defendant have taken precisely opposite initial strategies from those in our case. The court explains why it believes that the question of whether the defendant was negligent should go to the jury, even though the defendant's act appeared at first blush to be intentional.

TOPPS v. FERRARO

601 N.E.2d 292 (Ill. App. Ct. 1992)

Justice McLAREN delivered the opinion of the court:

The deposition testimony of the parties reveals the following facts. On June 28, 1987, plaintiff and defendant attended a social gathering at the home of a mutual friend. Shortly after the arrival of defendant and a female companion, defendant encountered plaintiff in the living room of the house and asked plaintiff if he would step outside for a moment to discuss something. Plaintiff, at that moment, did not feel challenged or threatened and agreed to step outside. Once outside, defendant asked plaintiff about earlier statements allegedly made by plaintiff about defendant's girl-friend. Within a short period of time, the conversation grew heated and argumentative.

In his deposition, plaintiff stated that he informed defendant that he would speak to him later after defendant calmed down. He said that he turned around and felt defendant touch his left shoulder, that the next thing he could recall was waking up one to two minutes later in the bushes with his left eye feeling sore, and that he smelled a strong odor of blood. Plaintiff stated that he could not recall any other details from the moment he turned around until he regained consciousness. He further stated that he did not remember whether he pushed or shoved the defendant.

At his deposition, defendant stated that after the argument became heated plaintiff shoved him in the shoulder, and he responded by punching plaintiff in the face, contacting plaintiff's left eye. Plaintiff then fell to the ground, stating that he required medical assistance. Defendant further testified:

A. [Defendant]: After talking and turning into an argument he pushed me on the shoulder, and once he hit me — well, pushed me, I hit him in the face. . . .

Q. So you said your reaction was to hit at him?

A. Well, that's just — I mean it wasn't something I thought about. Once he pushed me, I hit him, so it wasn't really any time.

Q. Is it your testimony at the time that you — that he pushed you it was your intent to hit him?

A. What?

Q. At the time —

A. He pushed me.

Q. It was your intent to hit him?

A. It wasn't a thought out thing. It was just all of a sudden I came up and hit him. . . .

Q. When you made contact with [plaintiff], what was your intention?

A. There was no intention. It was a matter — it was a matter of reflexes. I don't know what it was because really there was no time to think about it. Once he pushed me, I didn't think about he pushed me, hit him. It was just a matter of he pushed me and I hit him.

Q. Did you mean to hit him?

A. That was not — it wasn't my intention to bring him out there to go beat him up.

Q. I am saying at the time you did make contact?

A. Yes. There was no time. I didn't even think about it or anything. It was a matter of reaction.

The record does not reflect any additional testimony or factual evidence as to the altercation.

Plaintiff testified that at the time of his deposition, which was approximately three years after he sustained the injury, his field of vision was still impaired and that his visual acuity had further deteriorated.

~~In his one-count complaint plaintiff alleged:~~

4. . . . Defendant, Phillip Ferraro, was guilty of one or more of the following *negligent* acts:
   (a) Extended his arm in a *negligent* matter [*sic*] without due regard for the presence of others.
   (b) Made physical contact with the Plaintiff without due regard for the possible consequences of such contact.
   (c) Failed to keep proper lookout for the Plaintiff.
5. ~~That due to the foregoing *negligent* acts or omissions of the Defendant, Phillip Ferraro, the Plaintiff, Anthony Topps, was injured.~~ . . ." (Emphasis added.)

Plaintiff contends that an issue of material fact exists as to the "degree" of defendant's culpability and that the factual evidence presented in support of defendant's motion did not establish free and clear from doubt that defendant's conduct was other than negligent. Plaintiff focuses on defendant's professed state of mind at the time he struck plaintiff and argues that, because defendant was unable to provide an explanation why he struck plaintiff, a trier of fact could infer that defendant's conduct was negligent as opposed to intentional. Plaintiff further argues that defendant's testimony indicates that defendant negligently failed to contemplate the possible or probable consequences of his act in striking plaintiff. Defendant responds that the record clearly and unequivocally establishes that his actions were intentional and, therefore, no issue of material fact exists as to whether his conduct could be characterized as negligent.

Defendant argues that his intentional act precludes a grant of judgment to plaintiff on the issue of negligence by arguing the law relating to an intentional tort. However, defendant does not concede liability for either negligence or intentional tort because he claims self-defense. Defendant has failed to cite any law as to why an *un*reasonable belief in the need for self-defense is neither negligence nor an intentional tort. Defendant's argument, when distilled to its essence, is because he admitted that he committed an intentional *act*, he cannot be found to be negligent. Our independent research has disclosed two cases which allow recovery in negligence for such "intentional" acts. Blackburn v. Johnson, 543 N.E.2d 583 (1989); Wegman v. Pratt, 579 N.E.2d 1035 (1991).

In this case, plaintiff's complaint alleged the following *negligent* acts by defendant: "(a) Extended his arm in a negligent matter [*sic*] without due regard for the presence of others[,] (b) Made physical contact with the Plaintiff without due regard for the possible consequences of such contact[, and] (c) Failed to keep a proper lookout for the Plaintiff." To state a legally sufficient cause of action in either simple or willful and wanton *negligence*, plaintiff must have alleged sufficient facts to show defendant had a duty to plaintiff, that he breached such duty, and that an injury proximately resulted from that breach. [Wood v. Village of Grayslake, 593 N.E.2d 132 (1992).] The fact that defendant stated in his deposition that he intended to punch plaintiff neither mystically transmutes the allegations in plaintiff's complaint to an intentional tort nor precludes recovery in negligence.

The arguments of the parties set forth above are primarily due to the fact that the defendant apparently has insurance where coverage is dependent on the nature of the acts committed by defendant. The plaintiff has attempted to state a cause of action with facts that he believes will enable him to collect any judgment he might obtain. The defendant, on the other hand, has attempted to defend the action in such a way that no conflict of interest would arise between the defendant and his insurer. It is in this context that we consider whether the trial court erred in granting defendant's motion for summary judgment. . . .

We find that the pleadings, depositions, and admissions on file, together with the affidavits, reveal that there *is* a genuine issue of material fact regarding defendant's negligence regardless of the issue of intent or lack thereof. [*Blackburn*, 543 N.E.2d at 586; *Wegman*, 579 N.E.2d at 1043.] Accordingly, the trial court erred in ruling that no issue of material fact existed as to the nature of defendant's conduct as reasonable minds could find that the defendant was negligent in hitting the plaintiff.

For the foregoing reasons, we reverse the order of the circuit court of McHenry County granting judgment in favor of defendant, and the cause is remanded for further proceedings consistent with this opinion.

Reversed and remanded.

DOYLE, Justice, dissenting.

I respectfully dissent because I believe that the majority may have been led to an incorrect result through a misunderstanding of defendant's argument. The majority states that "[d]efendant's argument, when distilled to its essence, is because he admitted that he committed an intentional *act*, he cannot be found to be negligent" (emphasis in original) (601 N.E.2d at 294) and that defendant's admission in his deposition that he intended to punch plaintiff does not transform plaintiff's allegations into an intentional tort. I understand defendant's position to be that negligence is a theory of action which is separate and distinct from intentional tort and that, although plaintiff has elected to proceed on a specific theory of negligence only, the evidence before the trial court presented no issue of material fact as to whether defendant's conduct could be characterized as negligent within the allegations of the complaint.

Intent, as defined within the context of tort liability, is not necessarily a hostile intent, or a desire to do any harm; rather, it is an intent to bring about a result which will invade the interests of another in a way that the law will not sanction. [Cowan v. Insurance Co. of North America, 318 N.E.2d 315 (1974), citing W. Prosser, Handbook of the Law of Torts § 8, at 31 (4th ed. 1971).] Comment *b* of section 8A of the Restatement (Second) of Torts provides:

> All consequences which the actor desires to bring about are intended. . . . If the actor knows that the consequences are certain, or substantially certain, to result from his act, and still goes ahead, he is treated by the law as if he had in fact desired to produce the result.
>
> [Restatement (Second) of Torts § 8A, Comment *b*, at 15 (1965).]

The term "intent" is commonly used "to describe the purpose to bring about *stated physical consequences*" and is concerned with the consequences of the act. (Emphasis in original.) [W. Keeton, Prosser & Keeton on Torts § 8, at 35 (5th ed. 1984).] Motive focuses on the subjective rationale that inspires the act and the intent. W. Keeton, Prosser & Keeton on Torts § 8, at 35 (5th ed. 1984).

It is recognized that motive and intent are related states of mind and that confusion sometimes exists as to their precise interaction in the context of tort liability. In analyzing the circumstances of the present incident, however, I conclude that defendant's inability or failure in his deposition to specifically articulate his reason for striking plaintiff does not provide support for any inference that he acted negligently. Plaintiff's argument confuses motive with intent. Defendant's deposition testimony does not evidence his lack of intent; rather, it demonstrates his subjective reasoning, or lack thereof, as to why he engaged in an act of striking plaintiff. Although defendant testified that "it wasn't something he thought about" and that it was a matter of reflexes, he clearly and unequivocally stated that he struck plaintiff. The only reasonable interpretation of the evidence is that defendant struck out intentionally in response to allegedly being pushed by plaintiff.

Additionally, there is no evidence which suggests an alternative inference that defendant did not know or was substantially uncertain of the consequences of his act of striking plaintiff. Plaintiff has failed to respond to the motion for summary judgment by submitting facts which would raise an alternative inference [see Randle v. Hinckley Parachute Center, Inc., 490 N.E.2d 1041 (1986)], and he cannot rely upon mere conjecture or surmise as being sufficient to raise a genuine issue of negligence [see Koukoulomatis v. Disco Wheels, Inc., 468 N.E.2d 477 (1984)]. I conclude that the testimony relating to defendant's motive is insufficient to raise an issue of material fact as to whether defendant's conduct was negligent as opposed to intentional.

Intentional torts and negligence are distinct causes of action. Contrary to plaintiff's contention, differing theories of tort liability are distinguished, not by their difference in degree of culpability, but, rather, they are distinguished on the basis of their qualitative differences in kind. [See Burke v. 12 Rothschild's Liquor Mart, Inc., 593 N.E.2d 522 (1992) (qualitative differences between negligence and willful and wanton conduct preclude their comparison for comparative fault purposes).] Moreover, it is the presence of the recognized elements of negligence and not the absence of intentional or reckless conduct which determines the right to maintain a negligence cause of action.

If, from the evidence before the court, a plaintiff has failed to establish an element of his cause of action as alleged, summary judgment for the defendant is proper. [Pyne v. Witmer (1989), 543 N.E.2d 1304 (1989).] Plaintiff alleged his right to a cause of action based upon a specifically identified negligence theory of liability and was entitled to the benefit of every relevant fact necessary to succeed on that theory. His failure to provide sufficient evidence necessary to withstand defendant's summary judgment motion, however, required the trial court to determine, as a matter of law, that plaintiff was not entitled to maintain his cause of action for negligence.

For the foregoing reasons, I would affirm the circuit court's order granting summary judgment in favor of defendant.

QUESTIONS

1. Is it in the defendant's interest to deny that an intentional act can also be a negligent one? Why is the plaintiff in *Topps* taking a different approach from that of Mark against Joe? (Chapter 5 explores reasons why the defendant's interests and those of his insurance company may diverge here.)

2. Is there any set of plausible facts on which a negligence claim will succeed against Joe? Is there a way that Mark could prove negligence, even if Mark concedes that Joe's act of striking was intentional?

3. Suppose you represent Mark. How would you choose what claims to press in your complaint?

Another Point of Entry for Negligence in an Intentional Tort Case: Negligence by the Employer?

Mark sued not only Joe, but also the Cardinals organization for negligent hiring and negligent supervision. Mark's complaint averred that Joe had a reputation for violence before the Cardinals hired him as a coach; the Cardinals should have expected that he occasionally would be in some contact with the public, and therefore should not have hired him. Once the Cardinals did hire Joe, Mark claimed that they negligently failed to supervise Joe adequately to ensure that members of the public would not be harmed by him. As a result of the Cardinals organization's failure to exercise reasonable care in hiring and supervising their employees, the theory goes, Mark was harmed and should be compensated by the Cardinals.

When the Cardinals hired Joe to work as an assistant coach starting in 1996, he already had an established reputation in the league as being "mean." In 1980, the *New York Times* ran an article describing Joe's "reputation for meanness."[1] The article describes Joe's reputation in the National Football League and among members of the public. The incidents described include kicking and punching other players, resulting in fines, ejections, and reprimands by the NFL. In one highly publicized incident, Greene was caught by television cameras punching an opposing player in the stomach in retribution for numerous "dirty tricks" Joe felt the player had engaged in on the field. However, as the replay of the incident was shown dozens of times, fans saw only the punch and not the dirty tricks, and the image remained. It is perhaps this reputation the plaintiff hoped to invoke to build his case against the Cardinals for negligent hiring.

In preparing to argue the negligent hiring and negligent supervision claims, Mark's attorney deposed Michael Bidwill, vice president and general counsel for the Arizona Cardinals, and James McGinnis, who was the defensive coordinator for the Cardinals at the time of the incident.[2] In the following two excerpts, Mark's attorney asks Michael Bidwill about the team's hiring and disciplinary practices.

---

[1] William Barry Furlong, "Football Violence" *New York Times* (Nov. 30, 1980), 36.
[2] By the time his deposition was taken, James McGinnis was the head football coach for the Cardinals.

MICHAEL JOSEPH BIDWILL   04/25/2001

1

2

3   Q. (BY MR. ERICKSON) Would you then

4 expect a member of the Cardinals coaching staff

5 to react in such a fashion?

6   MR. KENNEDY: Form, foundation. Asked

7 and answered as well.

8   MR. BERK: Form.

9   THE WITNESS: No, I wouldn't expect

10 that any employee would have a reaction like

11 that, and no, I wouldn't expect it.

12   Q. (BY MR. ERICKSON) With respect to the

13 coaching staff, are you familiar with the range

14 of disciplinary actions that may be available to

15 the Cardinals if there is any particular instance

16 of malfeasance or misfeasance or inappropriate

17 conduct?

18   And I'm not talking about Mr. Greene in

19 particular, but generally speaking, are you

20 familiar with disciplinary actions that are

21 available to the Cardinals?

22   A. Yes.

23   Q. Would you tell me what those are,

24 please?

25   A. It can be all the typical forms of

MICHAEL JOSEPH BIDWILL   04/25/2001

21

```
 1  disciplinary action that range from warnings to,

 2  ultimately, dismissal.

 3       Q.  Is suspension also available?

 4       A.  Suspension would be available.

 5       Q.  Anything else that you're aware of?

 6       A.  You could require -- there's a range

 7  of things.  I mean, there are lots of things

 8  between that range.  But what my answer was

 9  before is those typical things would be available

10  for the organization.

11       Q.  Could the organization also require a

12  member of the coaching staff, for example, to go

13  through counseling?

14       A.  I believe so.

15       Q.  Could the organization fine an

16  individual?

17       A.  I think the organization could fine an

18  individual; although I'm guessing.  Let me say

19  I'm guessing at that.  I don't know for sure that

20  that's the case.

21       Q.  With respect to Mr. Greene and the

22  incident involving Mr. Cockriel, did the

23  organization impose any sort of discipline?

24            MR. KENNEDY:  Object to the form.

25            THE WITNESS:  Following the event, I
```

MICHAEL JOSEPH BIDWILL   04/25/2001

22

1   spoke with Joe and told him that, whether he was

2   right or wrong, he couldn't be involved in these

3   kinds of things.

4   And I had that conversation again with

5   him a few months ago when we extended his

6   coaching contract.

7   Q.   (BY MR. ERICKSON)   Had you ever had a

8   conversation like that with Mr. Greene prior to

9   the incident involving Mr. Cockriel?

10   A.   No, I had not.

11   Q.   So if we're talking about discipline,

12   would you consider the action that you took in

13   having those conversations with Mr. Greene to

14   have been a warning?

15   MR. KENNEDY: Objection to the form,

16   foundation.

17   THE WITNESS: Well, I consider the

18   conversation a conversation that he couldn't be

19   involved in things like that.   And I think if I

20   were to say -- you know, I just had that

21   conversation with him at both those occasions

22   that he couldn't be involved in things like that.

23   Q.   (BY MR. ERICKSON)   Do you consider that

24   to be a warning or not?

25   MR. KENNEDY: Same objection.

MICHAEL JOSEPH BIDWILL   04/25/2001

23

```
 1          MR. BERK:  Join.
 2          THE WITNESS:  I considered it to be a
 3  prospective sort of a warning, that in the future
 4  he couldn't be involved with these kinds of
 5  things.
 6          Q.  (BY MR. ERICKSON)  Was there any other
 7  disciplinary action taken, to your knowledge?
 8          A.  No.
 9          Q.  How did it come to be that you were the
10  one having that conversation with Mr. Greene
11  about not being involved in such incidents?
12          A.  Well, I am the person that was -- the
13  person who was approached on the field after the
14  incident and went to make sure that your client
15  got some medical care and had some familiarity
16  with it.  And I just decided to talk to Joe
17  Greene.
18          Q.  Now, does it fall within your job
19  description to discipline members of the coaching
20  staff?
21          A.  It falls within my job description to
22  discipline many members of our staff.  And,
23  again, I had this conversation with Joe Greene.
24
25
```

MICHAEL JOSEPH BIDWILL   04/25/2001

49

1   Q. Now, when you hire -- by "you" I mean

2 the Arizona Cardinals -- members of the coaching

3 staff, you expect those individuals to be known

4 on some level to the public, is that true?

5   A. Yes.

6   Q. You expect that they will have contact

7 with the public from time to time, is that true?

8   A. Yes.

9   MR. KENNEDY: Objection to the form.

10   Q. (BY MR. ERICKSON) And we've talked a

11 little bit about procedures for hiring, and you

12 may or may not know the answers to these

13 questions, and if you don't know, feel free to

14 say so.

15   But I take it, generally, the Cardinals

16 do have hiring policies and procedures, correct?

17   MR. KENNEDY: Objection to the form,

18 foundation.

19   THE WITNESS: When we hire people,

20 specifically with coaches, there's great

21 discretion given to the head football coach in

22 who he hires.

23   And there's no policy that's written.

24 There is -- commonly what happens is the head

25 football coach has great discretion in making an

MICHAEL JOSEPH BIDWILL   04/25/2001

50

1   independent, his own independent judgment about

2   who is the best -- who are the best coaches and

3   what positions they would fill that's going to

4   give him the opportunity to be successful.

5   Q.   (BY MR. ERICKSON)   As a matter of

6   standard practice, could the Cardinals do a

7   background check on potential candidates for

8   coaching positions?

9   MR. KENNEDY: Object to the form.

10   THE WITNESS: Well, what kind of

11 background check?

12   Q.   (BY MR. ERICKSON)   Any kind of

13 background check.

14   A.   Well, we don't do a criminal background

15 check, but we do do a -- we do ask about a

16 person's experience and what kind of coach they

17 were, if they were at another pro team or if they

18 were at a college.   We normally check with people

19 that have worked with them or they have worked

20 for, you know, and find out if they're a good

21 coach.   And so those sorts of things are done.

22 Yes.

23   Q.   So typically, you would do some sort

24 of -- make some sort of inquiry of personal or

25 character references, including people who may

MICHAEL JOSEPH BIDWILL   04/25/2001

51

```
 1    have worked with an individual in the past?

 2              MR. BERK:  Form.

 3              MR. KENNEDY:  Form.

 4              THE WITNESS:  They check into their,

 5    you know, professional experience, how they get

 6    along with the other staffs and things like that

 7    and what their work performance is.

 8              You know, good coaches are not just

 9    good and skilled at drawings of plays, but they

10    also have to motivate the players and have the

11    respect of players and work well with others, and

12    those are the sorts of things that are checked

13    out.

14         Q.  (BY MR. ERICKSON)  And to check that

15    out, typically, you would call people that they

16    had worked with in the past?

17         A.  I wouldn't call those people.  It would

18    be the head football coach or whoever he had

19    designated to start calling around.

20         Q.  Would the head football coach, or

21    others involved in the hiring decision, typically

22    read articles published in, for example, local

23    newspapers or national publications about an

24    individual?

25              MR. KENNEDY:  Form and foundation.
```

MICHAEL JOSEPH BIDWILL   04/25/2001

52

1   MR. BERK: Same objection.

2   MR. KENNEDY: Speculation.

3   Q.   (BY MR. ERICKSON)   If you know.

4   A.   I don't know what they did.   But I do

5   know that there is -- when you have a coaching

6   change, especially at this time, when we hired

7   Vince, it was February of '96.   There's a limited

8   pool of available assistant coaches out there.

9   And normally these -- most of your

10   staff is hired in one day or a day and a half or

11   two days.   And it happens very quickly because

12   there are other staffs that are getting secured.

13   And people are trying to figure out

14   where they're going to be from the employee side,

15   from the assistant coach side, and from the head

16   football coach's side or a coordinator's side,

17   they're trying to figure out who is going to be

18   on their staff and how fast they can fill it with

19   the best people because there are other teams out

20   there that typically have had coaching changes at

21   the end of the season that are snapping people

22   up, as well as colleges that are snapping people

23   up.   And so it's a fairly expeditious effort.

24

25

Below is an excerpt from the deposition of James McGinnis, who was the defensive coordinator for the Cardinals at the time the incident occurred.

JAMES DAVID MCGINNIS   04/25/2001

23

```
 1
 2        Q.  Did Mr. Greene tell you during the
 3   interview that because he has no opportunity for
 4   physical release of frustration as a coach,
 5   losing is harder for a coach than it is for a
 6   player?
 7        A.  During the interview, no.
 8        Q.  Has he ever expressed that thought to
 9   you at any other point in time?
10        A.  I don't -- I don't recall specifically
11   him ever saying that.  Possibly, but I don't
12   recall specifically.
13        Q.  Now, you were generally familiar with
14   Mr. Greene's reputation as a player, correct?
15        A.  Correct.
16        Q.  Back when he entered the NFL, I take it
17   you were still in college?
18        A.  Yes.
19        Q.  When you were in college, did you have
20   any involvement in football at the collegiate
21   level?
22        A.  Yes.
23        Q.  Did you play ball?
24        A.  Yes.
25        Q.  What positions did you play?
```

JAMES DAVID MCGINNIS   04/25/2001

24

1   A.   Defensive back.

2   Q.   Did you play all four years?

3   A.   Yes.

4   Q.   Do you recall in Mr. Greene's rookie

5   season -- I take it back. It wasn't his rookie

6   season. It was in the early '70s -- there was a

7   play-off game in Denver when Mr. Greene punched

8   out another player by the name of Paul Howard?

9   A.   No, sir.

10   Q.   Do you recall that feature story that

11 Sports Illustrated did about Mr. Greene in

12 September of 1975?

13   A.   No, sir.

14   Q.   You don't recall ever reading that?

15   A.   No.

16   Q.   It was reprinted, I think, in 1994. Do

17 you recall reading it then?

18   A.   No, I do not.

19   Q.   During your interview with Mr. Greene,

20 did he ever talk to you about uncontrolled anger

21 and fits of rage?

22   A.   No, he did not.

23   Q.   Did he ever talk to you about that at

24 any point other than in the interview?

25   A.   No.

1   Q.   Did he ever talk to you about the event

2   where he broke the teeth of one Bob DeMarco?

3   A.   No.

4   Q.   Have you ever talked to him about that

5   incident early in his career where he spit in

6   Dick Butkus' face?

7   A.   No, sir.

8   Q.   Did he ever talk to you about that

9   event during his rookie season where he kicked an

10   offensive guard in the groin in retaliation --

11   well, strike that.

12   Did he ever talk to you about that

13   event during his rookie season where he kicked an

14   offensive guard in the groin?

15   A.   No, sir.

16   Q.   Did he ever talk to you about incidents

17   in which he kicked open coolers because the water

18   boys or other staff were too slow in getting him

19   a drink?

20   A.   No.

21   Q.   Did you ever talk to him about whether

22   he considered himself to be a nice person?

23   A.   No.

24   Q.   During your interview with Mr. Greene,

25   I take it, from what you've testified to earlier,

```
 1    that your conversation was limited to a

 2    discussion of defensive philosophy and

 3    techniques, would that be a fair statement?

 4         A.  Yes, sir.

 5              MR. KENNEDY:  Object to the form,

 6    foundation.  Incomplete statement of what the

 7    testimony is.

 8              Go ahead, Dave.

 9         Q.  (BY MR. ERICKSON)  You never talked to

10    him about any particular events or incidents in

11    his past, did you?

12         A.  No, sir.

13         Q.  You never asked him about those

14    things?

15              MR. KENNEDY:  Objection to the form.

16    Misstates the prior testimony.

17              Go ahead.

18              THE WITNESS:  Not -- not in my part of

19    it.  No.

20         Q.  (BY MR. ERICKSON)  Are you aware of

21    anyone on behalf of the Cardinals asking

22    Mr. Greene questions relating either to specific

23    incidents in his past or his character?

24         A.  I'm not aware.

25
```

WRITTEN EXERCISE

Draft a brief memo outlining how negligence could be used in this case if *Topps* is the controlling precedent in the jurisdiction. Be sure to anticipate possible relevant differences between our case and *Topps*.

QUESTIONS

1. On the basis of the depositions, should the Cardinals be held liable for negligent hiring and/or negligent supervision? Should the claim at least survive summary judgment and get to a jury?
2. Would it make a difference if the Cardinals had taken disciplinary action against Joe *after* the incident occurred? Would that fact help or hurt the Cardinals in this case?
3. Suppose the Cardinals had required Joe to take anger management courses at some time prior to the accident. (This is completely hypothetical, of course.) Would this fact cut for or against Mark's negligent hiring/negligent supervision claim?

We review the outcome of a summary judgment motion by the Cardinals — asking to be dismissed from the case — in the next chapter. That chapter delves into vicarious liability, a theory of inclusion that, if its predicates are satisfied, requires no independent negligence by the Cardinals for effect. For the Cardinals to be dismissed from the case, they will have to show (under the facts as best construed in the plaintiff's favor) they were not negligent in hiring or supervising Joe — and that they were not vicariously liable for Joe's action that day on the field.

4

VICARIOUS LIABILITY AND INTENTIONAL TORT

THE BASICS

Vicarious Liability and Scope of Employment: Employers can be held liable for torts committed by an employee if the employee is acting "within the scope of employment" when he or she commits the tort. Employers are held vicariously liable based not on any fault of their own, but rather on the basis of their employment relationship with the alleged tortfeasor. The following section from the Restatement (Second) of Agency, describes factors often considered in determining whether a particular act was "in the scope of employment." (For those trying to nail down the doctrine, there are annoyingly subtle differences between the Restatement of Agency and the Restatement of Torts on the matter. Since neither controls, we offer only one summary here in order to give a flavor of the factors a court might consider.)

Kind of Conduct Within Scope of Employment (§ 229)

(1) To be within the scope of the employment, conduct must be of the same general nature as that authorized, or incidental to the conduct authorized.

(2) In determining whether or not the conduct, although not authorized, is nevertheless so similar to or incidental to the conduct authorized as to be within the scope of employment, the following matters of fact are to be considered:

(a) whether or not the act is one commonly done by such servants;

(b) the time, place and purpose of the act;

(c) the previous relations between the master and the servant;

(d) the extent to which the business of the master is apportioned between different servants;

(e) whether or not the act is outside the enterprise of the master or, if within the enterprise, has not been entrusted to any servant;

(f) whether or not the master has reason to expect that such an act will be done;

(g) the similarity in quality of the act done to the act authorized;

(h) whether or not the instrumentality by which the harm is done has been furnished by the master to the servant;

(i) the extent of departure from the normal method of accomplishing an authorized result; and

(j) whether or not the act is seriously criminal.

Restatement (Second) of Agency § 229 (1958).

Vicarious Liability ("Respondeat Superior") for Intentional Torts: An employer is typically only held liable for an employee's intentional tort when, authorized or not, the tort is committed in connection with the employee's employment and the act was "not unexpectable" in view of the duties of the employee. Restatement (Second) of Agency § 245 (1958).

> **Vicarious Liability Distinguished from Employer's Independent Negligence:**
> An employer may be liable for an employee's tort because of the employer's own
> independent negligence — such as negligently hiring or supervising the employee.
> This is a separate theory from the automatic imputation of vicarious liability that
> arises when the employee is acting within the scope of employment and, where
> required by law, to further the employer's interest.

As an initial matter, you may wonder why Mark's attorney would bother with
a claim against the Cardinals when there is a straightforward claim against Joe
who, after all, can be seen striking Mark on a videotape. Even if Mark succeeds at
trial and obtains a judgment against Joe, the game is not yet over. Mark now needs
to collect on the judgment, which will be difficult if Joe does not have sufficient
assets against which Mark can execute. It is more likely that the Cardinals (or the
Cardinals' insurance company) will have the assets to pay the judgment. This may
also benefit Mark because an employer may have less of an emotional stake in a
defendant-employee's "honor" in the case and therefore be willing to settle more
quickly if a cost-benefit analysis calls for settlement. On the other hand, compared
to Joe alone, the Cardinals may be better able to pay for a defense long enough to
prevail by simply "running the plaintiff out of money."

In Chapter 2 we focused on the development of facts even when they appear at
first blush to be straightforward. If Joe's actions were as they appeared to be in the
initial descriptions of the event, his conduct fell within the definition of assault and
battery. Therefore, in assessing the assault and battery case, the critical consideration
was whether Joe's conduct was really as it appeared. In this chapter, by contrast, many
of the relevant facts are undisputed. Joe is clearly an employee of the Cardinals, the
time and place of the incident are undisputed, and there are no major subjective
questions of intent to explore. The interesting questions here are questions of law.

To hold the Cardinals liable on a theory of vicarious liability (*i.e.*, on the basis
of their relationship with Joe, rather than on the basis of their own fault), Mark
must prove both that Joe engaged in tortious conduct and that Joe acted within
the scope of his employment when he did so. If the tortious act of the employee is
explicitly authorized by the employer, it is usually clear that the employer is liable.
Because striking Mark was certainly not specifically authorized by the Cardinals,
Mark will have to argue that the act was nonetheless in the scope of Joe's employment — and, if intentional, was "not unexpectable" — such an odd phrase! — in
view of Joe's duties as an employee.

One of the most influential factors in the determination of whether Joe's act
was within the scope of his employment is the starting and ending points of Joe's
"act." On the narrowest characterization of Joe's act — simply striking Mark — a
finding of *respondeat superior* seems unlikely. But on the broadest characterization
of Joe's act — coaching a football game and then leaving the field — a finding that
Joe acted in the scope of his employment seems more likely. The following two
cases show two courts discussing the definition of scope of employment in the
shadow of an intentional tort — the first, as a matter of doctrine; the second, as a
policy decision about whether to change the existing doctrine.

SAGE CLUB v. HUNT
638 P.2d 161 (Wyo. 1981)

BROWN, Justice.

Appellant, The Sage Club, appeals a judgment entered against it in a lawsuit arising out of an altercation between a bartender employed at the club, Mr. Thyfault, and a customer, appellee David Leland Hunt. The trial court entered a default judgment against Mr. Thyfault and held The Sage Club liable under the theories of respondeat superior and negligence in continuing to employ Mr. Thyfault. Appellant asserts that it cannot be held liable for the intentional tort of its employee because the tort was personal to Mr. Thyfault and was not within the scope of employment.

We affirm.

I

A dispute took place over money which appellee had left on the bar. Appellee thought that someone, supposedly Thyfault, had taken more money than he was entitled to take for his drinks. Mr. Thyfault undoubtedly resented the insinuation, so he jumped over the bar and attacked appellee. Thyfault hit appellee in the face, breaking his nose and inflicting other bruises, and then threw appellee down the stairs, reinjuring his back.

This court has held that an employer may be held liable for the negligent acts of an employee acting within the scope of employment, Gill v. Schaap, Wyo., 601 P.2d 545 (1979); Miller v. Reiman-Wuerth Company, Wyo., 598 P.2d 20 (1979); Combined Insurance Company of America v. Sinclair, Wyo., 584 P.2d 1034 (1978); and Stockwell v. Morris, 46 Wyo. 1, 22 P.2d 189 (1933). We have not, however, had occasion to rule on whether an employer may be held responsible for the intentional tort of an employee. The majority rule, in fact the universally accepted rule, holds employers liable for the intentional torts of employees committed within the scope of employment. Prosser, Law of Torts, § 70, p. 464 (4th ed., 1971). The rule is a matter of economic and social policy, based both on the fact that the employer has the right to control the employee's actions and that the employer can best bear the loss as a cost of doing business. The Restatement (Second), Agency 2d § 245, p. 537 (1958), phrases the rule as:

> A master is subject to liability for the intended tortious harm by a servant to the person or things of another by an act done in connection with the servant's employment, although the act was unauthorized, if the act was not unexpectable in view of the duties of the servant.

We agree with the accepted rule and hold that an employer may be held liable for the intentional tort of an employee if the employee is acting within the scope of employment. Appellant here contends that Mr. Thyfault was not acting within the scope of employment because the altercation which took place was a personal one between Thyfault and appellee. . . . We think the evidence here was sufficient to show that Thyfault was acting within the scope of employment when he attacked appellee. We said in Combined Insurance Co. of America v. Sinclair, *supra*, at 1041, that in general the servant's conduct is within the scope of his employment, "if it is of the kind which he was employed to perform, occurs substantially within the authorized limit of time and space, and is actuated, at least in part, by a purpose to serve the master," citing Prosser, Law of Torts, *supra*, p. 461 (4th ed.). Here, Mr. Thyfault's duties included collecting money for drinks, and he lost his temper over that matter. His duties also included keeping order in the bar and removing disruptive customers, which Thyfault apparently tried to do by pushing appellee down the stairs.

Appellant relies on Lombardy v. Stees, 132 Colo. 570, 290 P.2d 1110 (1956), for the proposition that since the assault was purely personal, it was not within the scope of employment. In that case, however, the evidence showed that the only express instruction to the bartender was that if anyone got too much to drink he was not to be served further. The bartender there had no authority to act as a bouncer; Thyfault did, and his employment was of such a nature as to contemplate the use of force. Indeed, the owner of The Sage Club testified that Thyfault sometimes had to remove people from the club on a daily basis.

In addition to the facts set out in Combined Insurance Co. of America v. Sinclair, supra, an important factor in deciding a principal's liability for his agent's intentional torts is whether "the use of force is not unexpectable by the master." Restatement (Second), Agency 2d § 228(1)(d), p. 504 (1958). Where the nature of the employment is such that the master must contemplate the use of force by the servant, the master will be held liable for the willful act of the servant even though he had no knowledge that the act would take place. Jones v. Herr, 39 Or. App. 937, 594 P.2d 410 (1979). The employer need not have foreseen the precise act or exact manner of injury as long as the general type of conduct may have been reasonably expected. Riviello v. Waldron, 47 N.Y.2d 297, 418 N.Y.S.2d 300, 391 N.E.2d 1278 (1979). Some who frequent grogshops are not the most docile members of society. Where an employee is serving in this type of environment as a bartender, the master is usually responsible if the employee loses his temper and willfully injures a patron because the result is foreseeable in view of the servant's job.

This court will therefore not indulge in nice distinctions to determine whether the excessive force was motivated by personal reasons. It is appellant's misfortune to have hired a quarrelsome and violent bartender who in turn attacked a plaintiff experienced at collecting on injury claims. Appellant evidently allowed Thyfault to use force at his discretion, and he was performing work of the kind he was employed to perform. The assault occurred within the authorized limits of time and space and was motivated, at least partially, by a desire to serve the Sage Club. Appellant is consequently vicariously liable to Mr. Hunt under the doctrine of respondeat superior. . . .

Affirmed.

[Dissent of THOMAS, J. omitted.]

KUEHN v. WHITE AND INTER-CITY AUTO FREIGHT, INC.
600 P.2d 679 (Wash. Ct. App. 1979)

CALLOW, Chief Judge.

The issue presented is whether the Washington rule which holds that an employer is not liable for an assault committed by an employee for his own purposes should be abandoned in favor of a rule which would impose liability on an employer when the employee injures a third party in a dispute arising out of the employment.

The facts are agreed upon by the parties. As the Kuehns' automobile proceeded down a hill, a truck tractor-semitrailer combination in the outside lane started to pass them. The truck was owned by Inter-City Auto Freight, Inc., and operated by Richard K. White. When the trailer of the combination pulled even with the Kuehns' automobile, the rig swerved left into the Kuehns' traffic lane. Mrs. Kuehn screamed "He's going to crash us. He's going to crash us." Mr. Kuehn applied his brakes and drove into the lane to his left.

Thereafter, Mr. Kuehn stepped on the gas, caught up with the truck, and motioned to White to pull over onto the shoulder of the highway. When the truck stopped, Kuehn parked behind it so that both he and Mrs. Kuehn could see the driver's door of the truck.

White got out of the cab of the truck and walked towards Kuehn's car carrying a 2-foot-long metal pipe owned by Inter-City. Mr. Kuehn got out of his car and asked White why he was carrying the pipe. White replied, "That's my equalizer." Mr. Kuehn asked White why he had attempted to force the Kuehns' automobile off of the road, to which White replied, "There is no son of a bitch going to give me the finger." White then swung the pipe at Kuehn's head, grazing the side of his face and knocking off Kuehn's glasses. As Kuehn bent over to pick up his glasses White hit him on the side of the head with the pipe, knocking Kuehn to his hands and knees, and when Kuehn tried to get up White hit him again on the head.

Mrs. Kuehn got out of the automobile and asked White, "What are you trying to do? Kill him?" White replied, "There's no son of a bitch going to give me the finger." White then got back into the truck and drove off, and Mrs. Kuehn took Mr. Kuehn to a hospital. Before this incident, White's record with his employer, Inter-City, had been good.

Later, White was convicted of assault. Mr. and Mrs. Kuehn then filed a civil action against White and Inter-City Auto Freight, Inc. Inter-City's subsequent motion for summary judgment of dismissal was granted. The Kuehns appeal.

A master is responsible for the servant's acts under the doctrine of respondeat superior when the servant acts within the scope of his or her employment and in furtherance of the master's business. Where a servant steps aside from the master's business in order to effect some purpose of his own, the master is not liable. [Citations omitted.]

If the assault by the servant is occasioned solely by reason of the servant's ill will, jealousy, hatred, or other ill feelings, independent of the servant's duty, then the master is not liable. E.g., Linck v. Matheson, 63 Wash. 593, 596, 116 P. 282 (1911). To fall within the scope of employment, the assault must be committed by authority of the employer, such authority being either expressly conferred or fairly implied from the nature of the employment and the duties incidental thereto as where the servant is authorized to maintain discipline or the character of the employment is liable to create disputes and result in breaches of the peace. An abuse or excessive exercise of the servant's authority in such situations does not relieve the master of liability. Langness v. Ketonen, *supra*, 42 Wash. 2d at 399-400, 255 P.2d 551; Brazier v. Betts, 8 Wash. 2d 549, 556-60, 113 P.2d 34 (1941).

Where the servant's intentionally tortious or criminal acts are not performed in furtherance of the master's business, the master will not be held liable as a matter of law even though the employment situation provided the opportunity for the servant's wrongful acts or the means for carrying them out. In Kyreacos v. Smith, *supra*, a Seattle police detective killed a man whom he suspected of murdering a complaining witness in a case in which the detective had arrested the decedent for a credit card forgery. The detective's conviction of first-degree murder was affirmed on appeal in State v. Smith, 85 Wash. 2d 840, 540 P.2d 424 (1975). In the subsequent wrongful death action brought by the decedent's widow, it was held that the City of Seattle was not liable under the doctrine of respondeat superior as a matter of law and that summary judgment was appropriate. The court stated that "if a servant steps aside from his master's business and, in order to effect some purpose of his own, commits an assault, the master is not liable." Kyreacos v. Smith, *supra*, 89 Wash. 2d at 429, 572 P.2d at 725. The court reasoned that the commission of premeditated murder by a policeman precluded any possibility that he was acting within the scope of his employment.

Recovery against the master has uniformly been denied in those instances where a servant-truck driver and the plaintiff collided, an altercation followed, and the driver lost his temper and struck the plaintiff. F. Harper & F. James, *supra*, § 26.9, at 1392 n.16; W. Prosser, *supra*, § 70, at 464. Accord, Restatement (Second) of Agency § 245, comment f, Illustration 8 (1958).

The plaintiffs urge an abandonment of these enunciated principles of respondeat superior. In their stead, the plaintiffs would have us embrace the rule adopted in California. Fields v. Sanders, 29 Cal. 2d 834, 180 P.2d 684, 172 A.L.R. 525 (1947); Pritchard v. Gilbert, 107 Cal. App. 2d 1, 236 P.2d 412 (1951). In those cases involving a servant's intentional assault, the California rule extends a master's liability to include risks inherent in or created by the enterprise for the reason that the master is thought to be best able to assume and spread the risk. A risk may be said to inhere in or be created by a business when "an employee's conduct is not so unusual or startling that it would seem unfair to include the loss resulting from it among other costs of the employer's business," or it is typical of the employer's business. Rodgers v. Kemper Constr. Co., 50 Cal. App. 3d 608, 124 Cal. Rptr. 143, 148-49 (1975). The risks of an employer's enterprise include those faults of human nature which may surface when a servant has contact with a third party. Carr v. Wm. C. Crowell Co., 28 Cal. 2d 652, 171 P.2d 5, 7-8 (1946). We note that the California rule is based in large part upon section 2338 of the California Civil Code, which makes a principal liable for the wrongful acts of the agent committed in and as a part of the principal's business. We find no comparable statutory directive in Washington and decline to impose a rule, the ramifications of which would be far-reaching and which would rearrange, across the state, the responsibility of employers for the conduct of their employees. Such a redirection of social policy is, more appropriately, the function of the legislature....

Here, as a result of White's driving, the Kuehns attempted to catch up with White's truck. Both then drove off the road. White then assaulted Kuehn because of his personal anger towards Kuehn and not because of any intent to serve the employer.

The judgment is affirmed.

FARRIS and RINGOLD, JJ., concur.

QUESTIONS

1. In the cases above, Thyfault and White each acted because they were personally offended or angry. Why does the court in *Sage Club* rule that Thyfault was acting within the scope of his employment while the court in *Kuehn* rules that White was not?

2. Consider the line in *Sage Club*: "Where an employee is serving in this type of environment as a bartender, the master is usually responsible if the employee loses his temper and willfully injures a patron because the result is foreseeable in view of the servant's *job*." (emphasis added)

    a. Does this mean that any action Thyfault takes is reasonably foreseeable because he is working in a rough environment?

    b. Is there anything Sage Club could have done to avoid liability for Thyfault's actions?

    c. Would the outcome of the case have been different if Thyfault had assaulted Hunt in the bar but not ejected him from the premises afterwards?

3. *Kuehn* notes, "[b]efore this incident, White's record with his employer . . . had been good."

    a. Why is this line in the opinion? Does it confuse a negligent hiring claim with a vicarious liability analysis?

    b. Would the *Sage Club* court have held differently if Sage Club had done a background check on Thyfault and it had come out clean?

    c. What amount of knowledge is the employer required to have about the violent nature or past actions of the employee to satisfy the doctrine of *respondeat superior*?

4. In *Kuehn*, why does the court note that White approached Kuehn's car "carrying a 2-foot-long metal pipe owned by Inter-City"? Of what significance is the fact that Inter-City owned the pipe?

WRITTEN EXERCISE

Compose a short memo analyzing the similarities and differences among Sage Club v. Hunt, Kuehn v. White and Inter-City Auto Freight, Inc., and the dispute between Mark, Joe, and the Cardinals. Which of the two cases is most similar to the dispute?

    One factor in a *respondeat superior* claim, explored in the above cases, is the breadth with which the "act" is characterized (*e.g.*, striking Mark vs. leaving a field after a game). Another important factor in the claim is the breadth or narrowness with which "employment" is characterized — what exactly are the duties of the alleged tortfeasor?

    In pressing the potential vicarious liability of the Cardinals, Mark's attorney used Joe's contract for employment with the Cardinals, and brought to bear the depositions of Michael Bidwill,[1] vice president and general counsel for the Arizona Cardinals, and James McGinnis, the defensive coordinator for the Cardinals at the time of the incident.[2] The relevant pages of Joe's employment contract are reproduced below, followed by a few deposition excerpts discussing the contract.

---

[1] There are some references in the deposition to Michael Bidwill's father, William Bidwill, the president of the Cardinals organization.

[2] By the time his deposition was taken, James McGinnis was the head football coach for the Cardinals.

3.   COACH agrees to devote all of his time to his duties assigned by the CLUB or the Head Coach during the entire term of this contract, provided that during the month of June, COACH shall be on vacation. COACH further agrees: (a) to keep himself in good physical condition; (b) to give the best of his talents, experiences and services and undivided loyalty to the CLUB and its team, and at all times to work for its best interests, and at no time during the term of this contract to have or agree to have in the future any financial interest in or connection or association with, directly or indirectly, any other football team, college or professional, as a coach or otherwise, without first obtaining the written consent of the President of the CLUB; (c) to conduct himself on and off the field according to the highest standards of honesty, morality, good conduct and sportsmanship; (d) to do nothing detrimental to the best interests of the CLUB, the National Football League or professional football; (e) to give his instructions to players and to work with other coaches of the CLUB in conformance with the policies prescribed by the Head Coach; and (f) as to all matters within the purview of this contract, to comply efficiently with and fulfill all reasonable requests and instructions of the CLUB.

COACH further agrees and acknowledges that, as an express condition of COACH's employment by the CLUB, COACH shall abide by all Rules and Regulations pertinent to COACH promulgated by the CLUB, as well as the provisions of any Employee Manual or guide which is currently in effect or which may be promulgated by the CLUB in the future. COACH must never sell a ticket to any CLUB or other National Football League game or to any other CLUB-sponsored or League-sponsored event for a price or other thing of value in excess of the face value of the ticket -- a practice commonly known as "scalping". COACH must not barter or trade tickets for personal gain or benefit, nor may COACH sell them for a price in excess of COACH'S cost. In any event, if tickets are provided to COACH for business use, COACH shall not convert them to personal gain or benefit or to the gain or benefit of his family or friends.

COACH acknowledges that the CLUB will not tolerate discrimi-
nation or sexual harassment of any kind, regardless of whether it
occurs in the work place or in other CLUB-sponsored settings.
COACH acknowledges that the CLUB strives to assure that no one is
burdened or wrongfully denied any opportunity on account of race,
color, religion, creed, sex, national origin, age or disability,
and that all individuals are treated with dignity and respect.
COACH hereby agrees that he shall indemnify and hold harmless the
CLUB from and against any claims, liabilities, or expenses
(including reasonable attorneys' fees) arising out of his wrongful
intentional conduct or out of any conduct of his which, due to its
grossly negligent or reckless nature, is treated as intentional
conduct under applicable law.

Is there anything within the contract's language that could be brought to bear on the issue of when Joe is on or off the job? Three excerpts from the Bidwill deposition are reproduced below that suggest an effort by the lawyers in this area. In the first excerpt, Mark's lawyer probes Bidwill's conception of the scope of Joe's employment with the Cardinals.

MICHAEL JOSEPH BIDWILL   04/25/2001

13

```
 1
 2
 3
 4
 5
 6
 7        Q.   (BY MR. ERICKSON)   Are you aware of
 8   whether your father has any particular set of
 9   criteria or prerequisites through which he
10   screens potential candidates when those names are
11   run by him?
12        A.   Well, I would imagine he does.  And,
13   you know, I don't know what all of those criteria
14   are.
15        Q.  As president of the company, is he the
16   final authority with respect to who gets hired
17   and who doesn't get hired?
18        MR. KENNEDY:  Objection to the form.
19        THE WITNESS:  He is the final authority
20   within our organization.  But every coaching
21   contract is approved by the commissioner's
22   office.
23        Q.   (BY MR. ERICKSON)  With respect to the
24   coaching staff of the Arizona Cardinals, would
25   you agree with me that when those individuals are
```

1   on the field at Sun Devil Stadium, they are

2   representing the team?

3   A.   When they're --

4   MR. KENNEDY: Object to the form.

5   THE WITNESS: -- on the field at Sun

6   Devil Stadium, they are -- on a game day, when

7   they're in their uniform around about the time of

8   the game, if they are acting within the scope of

9   their employment, they are representing the

10 Cardinals.

11   Q.   (BY MR. ERICKSON)   And how do you

12 define the scope of their employment?   What do

13 you mean by that term?

14   A.   Well, when he's doing his job duties,

15 he's within the scope of his employment.

16   Q.   Have you reviewed, at any point in

17 time, Mr. Greene's employment contract with the

18 Cardinals?

19   A.   Yes.

20   Q.   And the contract actually says, does it

21 not, that he is representing the Cardinals at all

22 times?

23   MR. KENNEDY: Are you representing that

24 that's a quote?

25   MR. ERICKSON: Well, if he doesn't

```
 1   recall that's what the contract says, he can

 2   answer in that fashion.

 3        MR. KENNEDY:  Well, object to the

 4   form.  And I'll just object to the form.  I think

 5   it's unfair to loosely use language and represent

 6   it as contract language without either indicating

 7   where the language is specifically taken from the

 8   agreement or showing the witness the agreement

 9   itself.

10        MR. ERICKSON:  Thank you, Mike.  If I

11   need an explanation on your form objections, I

12   will ask you.

13        Q.  (BY MR. ERICKSON)  Can you answer the

14   question as I stated it?

15        A.  I don't recall every line of each --

16   of the coachs' contracts.

17        Q.  Well, that doesn't answer my question.

18   My question was, do you recall that the contract

19   says that he is representing the Arizona

20   Cardinals at all times?

21        A.  No.

22        MR. KENNEDY:  Objection to the form.

23        THE WITNESS:  I do not recall that

24   specific language.

25
```

In this next excerpt from the Bidwill deposition, Bidwill discusses whether going on to and off of the field is, in his view, fixed "within the scope" of Joe's employment.

```
 1        Q.   (BY MR. ERICKSON)   Would you agree with

 2   me that if we go back to your original

 3   definition, which, as I understand it, is that a

 4   coach is acting within the scope of his

 5   employment when he is on the field at Sun Devil

 6   Stadium on a game day, when he's carrying out his

 7   coaching responsibilities, that he is also acting

 8   within the scope of his employment when he is

 9   entering or leaving the field?

10        MR. KENNEDY:   Object to the form.

11   Misstates prior testimony.

12        THE WITNESS:   I would say that while

13   he's on the field on game day, he's representing

14   the team, unless he's acting outside the scope of

15   his employment.

16        Q.   (BY MR. ERICKSON)   Do you view coming

17   and going -- strike that.

18        Do you view entering and exiting the

19   field as being within the scope of a coach's

20   employment?

21        MR. KENNEDY:   Form.   Legal conclusion.

22        THE WITNESS:   I view --

23        MR. KENNEDY:   Already asked and

24   answered.

25        THE WITNESS:   I view him being within
```

MICHAEL JOSEPH BIDWILL   04/25/2001

1   the scope of his employment as he comes and goes

2   off the field, as long as he's acting within the

3   scope of his employment.

4   Q. (BY MR. ERICKSON) Would you expect one

5   of your coaches to strike a member of the public

6   while on the field on game day?

7   MR. BERK: Form.

8   MR. KENNEDY: Form. Is that the end of

9   the question?

10   MR. ERICKSON: Yes.

11   MR. KENNEDY: Form.

12   THE WITNESS: No, I would not expect

13 that.

14   Q. (BY MR. ERICKSON) Would you expect a

15 member of the coaching staff of the Cardinals to

16 strike a member of the public anywhere?

17   A. No, I would not expect that.

18   Q. Have you watched the videotape of this

19 particular incident at any point in time?

20   A. Yes.

21

22

23

24

25

The following is the final excerpt of the Bidwill deposition in which the scope of employment issue is discussed.

MICHAEL JOSEPH BIDWILL   04/25/2001

53

1   A. The Cardinals have been in our family

2   since 1931.

3   Q. When did your father become president?

4   A. I believe it was 1972, maybe earlier

5   than that.

6   Q. Do the Cardinals, does the organization

7   have a subscription to Sports Illustrated?

8   A. I'm sure we do.

9   Q. The Cardinals have taken the position

10 in this litigation that Mr. Greene was acting

11 outside the scope of his coaching duties or other

12 employment with the Cardinals as a defense.

13   Can you tell me why you believe that

14 Mr. Greene was acting outside the scope of his

15 coaching duties when he was involved in this

16 incident with Mr. Cockriel?

17   MR. KENNEDY: Asked and answered,

18 form.

19   THE WITNESS: I believe I already

20 answered that, and I believe that it's our

21 position that anything -- you know, we don't

22 expect our employees to hit people or slap

23 people.

24   Q. (BY MR. ERICKSON) I take it you don't

25 authorize your employees to hit people?

MICHAEL JOSEPH BIDWILL   04/25/2001

54

1   A.   No, we do not.

2   Q.   And is that the reason that you think

3   Mr. Greene was acting outside the scope of his

4   employment in this particular situation?

5   MR. KENNEDY: Asked and answered, form.

6   THE WITNESS: We don't expect any of

7   our employees or authorize any of our employees

8   to be involved in any sort of violence, and that

9   includes Mr. Greene.

10   Q.   (BY MR. ERICKSON)   Well, and I don't

11   want to test Mr. Kennedy's patience, but is there

12   any reason for your belief that he was acting

13   outside of the scope of his employment in this

14   particular situation, other than the fact that he

15   hit Mr. Cockriel, that he was not authorized to

16   hit anyone?

17   MR. KENNEDY: It's an incomplete

18   statement of the testimony.   Form, foundation,

19   asked and answered.

20   THE WITNESS: At the time that

21   Mr. Greene slapped your client, I don't believe

22   he was acting within the scope of his employment

23   for the Cardinals.

24   Q.   (BY MR. ERICKSON)   Is there any reason,

25   other than the fact that he hit someone and he

MICHAEL JOSEPH BIDWILL   04/25/2001

1   was not authorized to hit someone, that you hold

2   that belief?

3   MR. KENNEDY: Same objections.

4   THE WITNESS: Could you restate the

5   question, please? I'm getting confused here

6   on -- we seem to be saying the same things, and

7   it's a little --

8   Q. (BY MR. ERICKSON) All I'm asking you

9   is if there is any other reason, any reason other

10   than the fact that he was not authorized to hit

11   someone, that you believe he was acting outside

12   the scope of his employment?

13   A. No.

14   MR. KENNEDY: Form, misstates, and it

15   is an incomplete statement of his prior testimony

16   on this subject.

17   Go ahead. I think you already have

18   gone ahead.

19   Q. (BY MR. ERICKSON) There's no other

20   reason that you're aware of that he was acting

21   outside the scope of his employment?

22   MR. KENNEDY: Same objections.

23   MR. ERICKSON: I think if I could get

24   one clear answer, we could be done.

25   MR. KENNEDY: Well, we've got a bunch

1 of clear answers. That's the problem. He's

2 given you a very long answer, and you're trying

3 to use abbreviated, shorthand versions. That's

4 the problem, and that's why the form of the

5 objection is appropriate.

6   Q.   (BY MR. ERICKSON) Mr. Bidwill, is

7 there any reason that you believe Mr. Greene was

8 acting outside the scope of his employment in

9 this situation, other than the fact that he was

10 not authorized to hit anyone?

11   MR. KENNEDY: Same objections.

12   THE WITNESS: It's that, plus I

13 would -- you know, the whole incident was very

14 unfortunate. And, you know, I would capsulize

15 that whole incident as something that may be

16 outside the scope of his employment or is outside

17 the scope of his employment and not something we

18 expected. Certainly, the slap is an important

19 part of that whole incident.

20   Q.   (BY MR. ERICKSON) Mr. Greene was

21 employed by the Cardinals on October 31st, 1999,

22 correct?

23   A.   Yes.

24   Q.   He was on the field at Sun Devil

25 Stadium when this incident occurred because that

MICHAEL JOSEPH BIDWILL   04/25/2001

57

```
 1   was part of his job, right?
 2           MR. KENNEDY:  Objection.  Object.
 3   Objection to the form.
 4           THE WITNESS:  He was exiting the field
 5   following the game.
 6           Q.  (BY MR. ERICKSON)  And he was on the
 7   field during the game because that's part of his
 8   job, correct?
 9           A.  Yes.
10           MR. ERICKSON:  All right, sir.  Thank
11   you for your time.  I don't have any further
12   questions.  I don't know if Mr. Berk has
13   questions.
14           MR. BERK:  I do not.
15           MR. KENNEDY:  We'll read and sign.
16           (The deposition concluded at 10:06
17   a.m.)
18
19
20
21
22
23
24
25
```

In deposing defensive coordinator McGinnis, Mark's lawyer inquired about provisions in the employment contract that might shed light on the scope of employment. The relevant discussion from the deposition is reproduced below.

JAMES DAVID MCGINNIS   04/25/2001

27

```
 1

 2

 3        Q.  I take it you've probably never seen

 4   Coach Greene's contract, is that true?

 5        A.  I've -- I've seen the contracts and an

 6   assistant coach's contract.  I have one.

 7        Q.  Do you recall a provision in that

 8   contract that calls for a coach to devote all of

 9   his time to the duties assigned by the club, to

10   give the best of his talents, experiences, and

11   services to the club, and at all times to work

12   for the best interests of the club on and off the

13   field?

14             MR. KENNEDY:  Object to the form,

15   foundation.

16             (Mr. Bidwill exited the deposition

17   room.)

18             THE WITNESS:  Yes, sir.  That is in the

19   contract.

20        Q.  (BY MR. ERICKSON)  Coach Greene was on

21   the field at Sun Devil Stadium on October 31st,

22   1999, because he was an assistant coach to the

23   Cardinals, correct?

24        A.  Correct.

25        Q.  And, well, would you expect a member of
```

JAMES DAVID MCGINNIS   04/25/2001

28

```
 1   your coaching staff to hit or strike a member of
 2   the public while on that field?
 3             MR. BERK:  Form.
 4             (Mr. Bidwill entered the deposition
 5   room.)
 6             THE WITNESS:  Not of that -- an action
 7   like that is not what I expect anywhere.
 8        Q.  (BY MR. ERICKSON)  Right.  And you
 9   wouldn't expect them to strike a member of the
10   public while on that field for any reason,,
11   correct?
12             MR. BERK:  Form.
13             THE WITNESS:  Correct.
14        Q.  (BY MR. ERICKSON)  Have you watched the
15   videotape of this incident?
16        A.  No, sir.
17        Q.  Have you had any conversations with
18   Mr. Greene about the incident?
19        A.  No.  Just the day after I asked him if
20   there was an incident, and he said yes.  And then
21   I basically just let it go.
22        Q.  And why did you let it go?
23        A.  Well, because I asked him, and he said
24   there was really -- he didn't -- he didn't
25   divulge, nor go into it, so I didn't pursue it.
```

QUESTIONS

1. Why do the attorneys object with such frequency to the questions posed to the witnesses during the depositions? Why should the witnesses be required to answer the questions even though counsel believes the questions are phrased improperly? Are there strategic objectives, other than ensuring proper phrasing of the questions, that counsel may have in mind when making these objections?

2. What other techniques and methods can attorneys use to gather information during the discovery process? What are the advantages of deposing a witness in person as compared to these other methods? What are the disadvantages?

WRITTEN EXERCISE

Choose one person in this action and draft a set of interrogatories designed to elicit information from that person. Keep in mind the relative advantages and disadvantages of interrogatories and design your questions accordingly.

It is important to distinguish the vicarious liability claim discussed in this chapter from the negligent supervision and negligent hiring claims discussed in Chapter 3. The negligent supervision and negligent hiring claims required proof of fault on the part of the Cardinals. The negligence was asserted directly against the Cardinals. By contrast, the vicarious liability claim discussed in this chapter is a claim of *indirect* liability against the Cardinals; their liability arises through Joe's actions. In order to prove the vicarious liability against the Cardinals, Mark need not prove any fault on the part of the Cardinals, but must prove that Joe, as a Cardinals employee, committed a tortious act.

QUESTIONS

1. If you were the judge in this case, would you find that the Cardinals are subject to vicarious liability? Is this an issue properly left to the jury — so long as reasonable jurors could disagree — or is it a question of law for the judge to resolve?

2. In the summary judgment opinion finding that the facts could not support independent liability for the Cardinals on a negligent hiring or supervision theory, the trial judge found that Joe's conduct was not something he had been hired to perform, and that it did not have a purpose to benefit his employer. Does this mean that it would not matter whether the altercation happened after the game was over, during halftime, or even during the game itself?

3. If a theory of negligence had been pled, would it have affected the analysis of the Cardinals' vicarious liability?

4. What legal position should Joe take regarding the potential vicarious liability of the Cardinals?

5

INSURANCE: THE GAME BEHIND THE GAME

THE BASICS

Duty to Indemnify: Liability insurance policies obligate insurance companies to indemnify insureds — to pay others' valid legal claims against the insured, up to the amount of the policy limit, for those claims that are within the scope of the insurance policy's coverage. The duty to indemnify (or to "cover the loss") arises when an injured party's claim against the insured has been transformed into a judgment or when the parties (including the insurance company) have agreed to a settlement of the injured party's claim.

Duty to Defend: Liability insurance policies typically obligate insurance companies to provide a defense — that is, to provide a lawyer who will defend the insured, when the claims made in the complaint fall within the scope of the insurer's coverage or the pleadings of the case are such that there are factual allegations against the insured that support claims that *could be* within the scope of the insurance policy's coverage. The duty to defend is thus broader than the duty to indemnify, since the duty to indemnify arises only once a claim against the insured is reduced to judgment or settlement and is determined to be within the scope of the insurance policy.

Reservation of Rights: An insurance provider defends under a "reservation of rights" when it agrees to provide a defense for an insured defendant but reserves the right to contest its duty to indemnify the insured for damages that may be awarded in the lawsuit. This happens when it appears to the insurance company that the plaintiff's claims will fall outside the policy's coverage even if valid, but there remains some doubt about that assessment, perhaps because of legal or factual uncertainty still to be resolved within the litigation process.

Intentional Harm Exclusion: Most liability policies contain language excluding from coverage harm arising from an intention to cause harm by the insured. Moreover, most states insist on such exclusion by refusing to enforce more expansively written policies, on the theory that intentional wrongdoers ought to bear the full financial brunt of the consequences of such conduct.

Glossary of Participants:

Gulf Insurance (and their umbrella group, Select Insurance): Providers of liability insurance for the Cardinals, the team that employs Joe Greene.
Farmers Insurance: The providers of Joe Greene's homeowners' insurance.
Lester E. Zittrain: Joe Greene's personal attorney.
Robert Berk and William Holm: Attorneys appointed by Gulf Insurance to represent Joe.

PART A: DO YOU NEED A LAWYER TO GET A LAWYER? — DUTY TO DEFEND, DUTY TO INDEMNIFY, AND THE SCOPE OF INSURANCE

On April 14, 2000, Joe received a letter that said, in essence, "Pay me $100,000 by 5 P.M. on April 28, or I'll file papers to sue you for assault and battery." His immediate response was, not surprisingly, that he needed an attorney to help him respond and, if necessary, defend him in the suit. He called his personal attorney, Les Zittrain, who had represented Joe on his employment and endorsement contracts over the years. Zittrain then got in touch with insurance companies whose policies might be implicated: Farmers, Joe's homeowner's insurance, which provided a policy that included "umbrella liability" indemnity for many types of third-party claims; and Gulf/Select, which provided liability insurance to the Cardinals and perhaps to the team's employees. He asked them not only for indemnification, but also to provide an attorney for Joe's defense in the case.

Why should Joe need a lawyer to convince the insurance companies to provide a lawyer for him? The textbook model for dealing with a pending claim is for the defendant simply to call his or her insurance company to report the claim, after which a lawyer is appointed. Here Joe's personal lawyer began the process of alerting not one but two insurance companies whose policies were potentially implicated — and undertook to convince each that a defense was indeed called for by the policies.

The facts of the case — foremost, the claimed and, at first blush, apparent desire to cause harm by Joe — make denial of coverage a somewhat tempting option for the insurance companies. Intentional harm by the insured are excluded from coverage by both the language of almost all insurance policies and common law declaring insurance of intentional harm void as against public policy. The public policy rationale is based on the dangers of allowing people to insure themselves against liability for intentional harm and then feeling free to commit battery, fraud, and many other unsavory acts, secure in the knowledge that they will not personally have to pay any judgment that results. It also flows from the idea that insurance is a hedge against risk by the insured — and that intentional harm is typically freely chosen rather than accidental. (Negligence, of course, also has a flavor of choice — we say what a defendant "ought" to have done in retrospect — but one could still imagine hewing to an analytic distinction along the spectrum of intent.)

When determining how to react to an insured's filing of a claim, the insurance company must make two analytically separate but factually related coverage decisions. The first decision is whether the insurance company has a duty to provide a lawyer to defend the insured. The second decision is whether the insurance provider is required to indemnify the insured — to pay on the insured's behalf if the plaintiff succeeds in proving the claims. The two decisions need not be made at the same time. An insurance company can elect to provide a defense under a reservation of rights, which allows the company to defend the insured while preserving its ability to contest its obligation to indemnify the insured. If the plaintiff's claims prove meritless or the plaintiff wins only on claims outside the scope of the insurance policy, the insurance provider may provide a defense but ultimately not be required to indemnify the insured.

An insurance company's duty to defend cuts a fairly wide swath, requiring the insurance provider to defend if the claims alleged in the complaint are covered within the policy or if the facts of the case could support a claim that would be within the scope of the policy. These are distinct from one another, which has led to some doctrinal uncertainty: What if a plaintiff alleges only intentional tort, but the facts underlying the claim would support a claim of negligence? What if the facts appear to support an intentional tort, but the plaintiff asserts negligence?

One question for the insurance companies, then, is whether any nonintentional, covered claim can be culled from the still-to-be-developed facts even though Mark's initial complaint alleged only intentional tort. As Chapter 3 describes, one outcome (and arguably the most plausible one) of a finding that Joe's act was not intentional is that Joe is simply not liable on the theory that his conduct does not constitute an "act" of the kind required for liability in either intentional tort or negligence. Thus, an insurance company analyzing the case might look at the possibilities as (1) the claim is based on an intentional harm, therefore no coverage; or (2) the act was non-intentional, and the claim is therefore meritless because there was no "act." Of course, a meritless claim still must be defended against, and one can imagine a legitimate desire to obtain insurance so as to have a lawyer to defend against all types of claims, not allowing the plaintiff's choice of pleadings alone to determine whether the defendant gets a lawyer.

How should the insurance company respond to the possibility that the claim is meritless? There are two possibilities. First, if the facts as described by either side do not appear to give rise to a covered claim, *and no such claim is alleged* by the plaintiff, the insurance company may refuse to provide a defense. In refusing, the insurance company is not acting entirely without risk. In this case, however, the insurance provider is taking only the risk that facts will emerge that ultimately support the finding of a covered claim (such as garden-variety negligence) and such a claim will be asserted against the defendant, leaving the insurance company open to a claim of failure to defend by the defendant. In the alternative, if the insurance company can see no covered claim arising from the facts of the case, *but the plaintiff has nonetheless made such a claim* that falls within the scope of the policy, the insurance company is generally thought to be obliged to defend on the basis of even the meritless claim.[1]

Note that the way in which this duty arises gives the plaintiff some limited degree of control over whether the defendant will be able to procure a defense from his insurance company. If the plaintiff's complaint includes a claim covered by the insurance policy, the insurer will be obligated to provide a defense even if the plaintiff's claim is meritless. On the other hand, if the plaintiff's complaint includes only claims of intentionally-inflicted harm, it will be more difficult for the defendant to convince his insurers to provide a defense for him. The plaintiff's strategic determination regarding whether he will fare best with or without the defendant's insurance provider involved in the suit therefore may affect which claims the plaintiff

---

[1] For more on this issue, see Stephen S. Ashley, *Bad Faith Actions: Liability and Damages* § 4:4 (2d ed. 1997); William M. Shernoff, Sanford M. Gage, & Harvey R. Levine, *Insurance Bad Faith Litigation* § 3.10[3][b] (2002).

asserts, and in turn, which facts the plaintiff seeks to develop. The defendant, too, may seek to develop facts that could compel coverage — not every intentional *act* falls within a policy's intentional harm exclusion.

Further, intentional harm is not the only basis on which to determine a policy's coverage; there are plenty of other factors listed in a policy designed to sketch its boundaries. Because the incident took place on the football field following a game in which Joe was working as a coach, and because the Cardinals were already involved in the lawsuit as named defendants, Joe sought insurance coverage and a defense from his employer's insurer, Gulf/Select, as well as from his own homeowner's insurance carrier, Farmers.

PART B: HOW THE GAME IS PLAYED — FENCING WITH INSURANCE

As soon as Joe was put on notice of a possible claim against him, he worked to convince the insurance companies to provide a defense. The companies explained the rationale for their coverage decisions in letters responding to Joe and his attorney. Gulf's decision arrived before Farmers', and was expressed in the following letter.

Gulf Insurance Group
A member of citigroup

May 24, 2000

Les Zittrain, Esq.

CLAIM NUMBER:	
INSURED:	B & B HOLDINGS, INC.
	DBA ARIZONA CARDINALS
DATE OF LOSS:	10/31/99
CLAIMANT:	MARK COCKRIEL

Dear Mr. Zittrain:

This letter will formally acknowledge the receipt of the Mark Cockriel claim against both the Arizona Cardinals and Joe Greene and to advise your client, Joe Greene, of Select Insurance Company's coverage position for this matter. We would ask that you forward a copy of this letter to Mr. Greene for his review.

As we discussed on May 9, 2000, there are two distinct coverage issues as they relate to the Cockriel claim that has been made against Mr. Greene. Outlined below you will find Select Insurance Company's analysis of the coverage available to your client under the insurance policy issued to the Arizona Cardinals.

Mark Cockriel has made a claim against Joe Greene, arising out of a post-game incident on October 31, 1999. In a demand letter of April 14, 2000, Mr. Cockriel, through his attorney, claimed that Joe Greene intentionally assaulted him on the evening of October 31, 1999 and has demanded $100,000, and an apology from Mr. Greene, for damages arising out of that assault. A complaint has been drafted, but not yet filed or served, against both the Arizona Cardinals and Joe Greene asserting that Joe Greene deliberately and viciously struck Mr. Cockriel in the head, causing bodily injury and emotional distress. In addition, based on the allegations of intent and malice, Cockriel prays for punitive damages.

When reviewing claims for coverage under the insurance policy, Select Insurance makes no judgment as to the truth or falsity of the allegations. Select looks only to determine if coverage could potentially apply if the allegations were proven.

Select Insurance Company issued a contract of insurance to, among other entities, B & B Holdings, Inc., dba Arizona Cardinals. This policy,   was effective from February 1, 1999 to February 1, 2000. One of the sections of this policy provides the

Gulf Insurance Group

May 24, 2000
Page 2

named insured with General Liability coverage. The primary insuring agreement, for this coverage, is the Commercial General Coverage Form (CG0001 Ed. 01/96). This coverage form provides under Section I. Coverage A., Bodily Injury and Property Damage Liability coverage and under Section I., Coverage B., Personal and Advertising Injury Liability Coverage.

Although the coverage provided by this insuring form is quite extensive, it is not unlimited. As with all insurance policies, certain exclusions or limitations might be applicable to any given set of facts surrounding a claim that has been presented under the policy. This is the case in the claim, as presently presented, of Mark Cockriel against Joe Greene.

First, as noted above, the Select policy was issued to B & B Holdings, Inc., dba Arizona Cardinals. They are the named insured. In Section II. – Who Is An Insured, the policy defines who else might qualify for coverage as an insured, under the Arizona Cardinals policy. In 2. a. of this section, "employees" are insureds under the policy, but "only for acts within the scope of their employment by (the named insured) or while performing duties related to the conduct of (the named insured's business)." Although Mr. Greene may have been in the course of employment, the Arizona Cardinals will undoubtedly assert that the act of striking Mark Cockriel was certainly outside the scope of his employment. Accordingly, unless there is a finding that Mr. Greene was acting within the course and scope of this employment with the Arizona Cardinals, no coverage would exist under their policy for this claim.

Further, as Cockriel is asserting that Mr. Greene intentionally struck him, Select would refer you to the insuring agreement for Bodily Injury and Property Damage Liability, found in Section I., Coverage A. Although this agreement covers damages due to "bodily injury" or "property damage" (as defined in the policy), it requires that the "bodily injury" or "property damage" be caused by an "occurrence". "Occurrence" is defined as an . . . "accident". As fortuity is the foundation of insurance, the importance of this requirement is reinforced in 2. Exclusions. The first exception to coverage is that for a. Expected or Intended Injury, which excludes coverage for "bodily injury" or "property damage" expected or intended from the standpoint of the insured . . . .

The Arizona courts have generally found that a presumption exists that there was an intent to harm when an act is intentional and when the injury results from a natural and probable consequence of this intentional act, notwithstanding the subjective intent of the actor. As such, should a jury, or other finder of fact, determine that the actions of Mr. Greene were intentional in nature, it is extremely doubtful that Select Insurance would have a duty to respond to any award for damages arising out of that intentional act.

As indicated above, this policy also provides coverage for "personal injury" and "advertising injury" liability. None of the allegations, however, qualify as "personal injury" or "advertising injury" as these terms are defined in the policy.

May 24, 2000
Page 3

Although Select Insurance Company believes that there is little possibility that we would owe a duty to pay any damages that might be awarded for Mr. Cockriel's injuries, the policy of insurance also has a separate duty of defense. After reviewing the facts of this claim, Select Insurance Company does believe it would owe a duty to defend Mr. Greene and will do so, defending the claim in its entirety. Select Insurance, however reserves it right to withdraw from the defense of Joe Greene, at any time, should we feel that the potential for coverage no longer exists.

Conditioned on the above, Select Insurance Company will investigate and provide a defense of this claim. Any investigation or other action taken by Select Insurance Company, or any of its representatives, is done, with Select Insurance Company reserving all the rights under the policy of insurance. Specifically, the investigation and defense of this claim does not constitute a waiver of any rights that Select Insurance Company may have under the policy and Select Insurance Company will enforce all terms, conditions, provisions and exclusions of the policy. Of course, it is understood that Joe Greene is not waiving any of his rights under the policy by accepting defense under this reservation of rights.

In line with this, we discussed the possibility that Gulf Insurance, in concert with Farmers Insurance Company, Mr. Greene's personal liability carrier, may attempt to settle this claim if this can be done in a cost effective manner. Select Insurance Company would emphasize that any offer of settlement, once again, is not intended to be a waiver of any rights that may exist under the policy.

Should you have any questions regarding this letter, or believe our coverage position is in error, please do not hesitate to contact me or provide me with any additional information you believe may affect our coverage analysis. I have provided a copy of the Arizona Cardinals declaration pages and the primary insuring form for your review.

Finally, I would like to inquire as to Mr. Greene's position regarding the apology to Mr. Cockriel. If settlement of this claim could be made in a cost effective manner, that is contingent upon an apology from Mr. Greene, it is imperative that we know what Mr. Greene's position will be in this matter.

Sincerely,

Beverly J. Miller
Claim Manager
Dallas Specialty Claims
Select Insurance Company,
Member of Gulf Insurance Company

BJM/lj

It appears here that Gulf has agreed to provide a defense for Joe under a "reservation of rights." Note that Gulf reserved not only the right to refuse to indemnify Joe, but also the right to withdraw the defense in the middle of the litigation if facts came to light (or simply became more certain) that would lead Gulf to conclude that it would manifestly not owe indemnification if Joe were found liable.

This left both Joe and his soon-to-be-assigned insurance-paid attorney in a some-what precarious position: Joe will have an insurance company-provided lawyer that could be taken off the case at any point down the line, leaving Joe to find (and personally fund) another lawyer to quickly familiarize herself with the case and pinch hit. The insurance company-appointed lawyer could in turn face tough dilemmas as the litigation progresses, since so much of the process involves developing and proving facts that are uncertain. How should a lawyer who represents Joe, is paid by the insurance company, and will stay in the case only so long as there remains a claim covered by the insurance company, seek to establish and portray facts that could release the insurance company from its obligation to provide a defense? (Recall the *Topps* case in Chapter 3.) How can the lawyer best act in Joe's interest? Does the lawyer have any obligation to the insurance company that is paying his bills?

QUESTIONS

1. How many and what sort of rationales does Gulf provide for its reticence to fully defend Joe?
2. Do you think that this response by Gulf Insurance is generous to Joe?
3. How would you respond to this letter if you were Joe's attorney?
4. Note the description of the insurance provider's method of determining coverage on the first page of the letter: "When reviewing claims for coverage under the insurance policy, Select Insurance makes no judgment as to the truth or falsity of the allegations. Select looks only to determine if coverage could potentially apply if the allegations are proven." Does this mean that whether the insurance company will provide a defense is determined by the way the *plaintiff* phrases the complaints? For more on this issue, see Ellen S. Pryor, "The Stories We Tell: Intentional Harm and the Quest for Insurance Funding," 75 Tex. L. Rev. 1721 (1997).

Joe's personal lawyer responded to Gulf's coverage position with the following letter.

LAW OFFICES

ZITTRAIN AND ZITTRAIN

ATTORNEYS AT LAW

201 FRANKLIN PROFESSIONAL BUILDING

4240 GREENSBURG PIKE

PITTSBURGH, PA 15221-4235

LESTER E. ZITTRAIN*
RUTH A. ZITTRAIN**

*ALSO ADMITTED IN VIRGINIA
**ALSO ADMITTED IN FLORIDA

TELEPHONE
(412) 271-2200

FAX
(412) 271-2300

May 31, 2000

Beverly J. Miller, Claim Manager

Re:	Claim Number:	
	Insured:	B & B Holdings, Inc.
		DBA Arizona Cardinals
	Date Of Loss:	10/31/99
	Claimant:	Mark Cockriel

Dear Ms. Miller:

This will acknowledge receipt of your letter of May 24, 2000 pertaining to Joe Greene and the captioned matter.

I have, of course, read your letter and your position therein relative to coverage. However, presently I do not feel it is my obligation to analyze either the relevant Select Insurance Company policy or Arizona case law so as to determine at this time whether or not I believe your coverage position is in error. That bridge can be crossed, if necessary, at a later time.

Your letter has been forwarded on to Mr. Greene.

In the meanwhile, please keep me apprised of all developments in the claim as they occur.

Sincerely,

LESTER E. ZITTRAIN

LEZ: dmb

cc: Joe Greene

QUESTION

Why would Joe's personal attorney not express a view regarding Gulf's decisions regarding coverage?

Recall that in addition to seeking coverage from his employer's insurance carrier, Joe asked his homeowner's insurance provider, Farmers, to provide a defense and indemnification. Relevant provisions of Joe's homeowner's insurance policy are reproduced below. As you read the provisions, try to predict what position Farmers will take, given what you know about the position taken by Gulf in the matter.

SECTION II — LIABILITY
Coverages
Coverage E — Personal Liability

We will pay those damages which an **insured** becomes legally obligated to pay because of **bodily injury, property damage** or personal injury resulting from an **occurrence** to which this coverage applies. . . .

SECTION II — EXCLUSIONS
Applying To Coverage E — Personal Liability

We do not cover:

     2. Punitive or exemplary damages or the cost of defense related to such damages.

Applying to Coverage E and F—Personal Liability and Medical Payments to Others

We do not cover **bodily injury, property damage** or personal injury which:
     1. arises from or during the course of **business** pursuits of an **insured**. . . .
     3. is either:
          a. caused intentionally by or at the direction of an **insured**; or
          b. results from any **occurrence** caused by an intentional act of any
            insured where the results are reasonably foreseeable.

QUESTIONS

1. According to this policy excerpt, is Farmers obligated to provide a defense for Joe?
2. Is Farmers obligated to indemnify Joe?
3. What factors shape Farmers' decision that did not apply to Gulf's decision? What factors apply to the coverage analysis for both Farmers and Gulf?

As explained in the letter below, unlike Gulf, Farmers opted to deny coverage altogether. Whereas Gulf provided a defense for Joe while reserving its right to refuse to indemnify if it finds that the claim is not covered, Farmers denied both indemnification and a defense.

 **FARMERS**

1365 S. Gilbert Road
P.O. Box 8640
Mesa, AZ 85214-8640

www.farmerinsurance.com

July 20, 2000

Charles Greene

RE: Insured   :
             Policy No.   :
             Loss Date   :
             Claimant   :
             Claim No.   :

Dear Mr. Greene:

Thank you for your patience in allowing us to review the coverage aspects of your claim. A review of the information available to us at this time reveals that you had just completed coaching an Arizona Cardinals football game. You were walking off the when the claimant, operating a four wheel ATV type vehicle, ran over your foot, prompting you to strike the claimant in the head. We would direct you to your Protector Plus Homeowners Policy which states in part:

AGREEMENT
We will provide the insurance descried in this policy. In return you will pay the premium and comply with all policy conditions.

DEFINITIONS
Throughout this policy, "you" and "your" mean the "named insured" shown in the Declarations and spouse if a resident of the same household. "We," "us" and "our" mean the Company named in the Declarations which provides this insurance. In addition, certain words appear in bold type. They are defined as follows:

> . . . 4. **Bodily injury** — means bodily harm, sickness or disease, including care, loss of services and death resulting from that injury.

> . . . 5. **Business** — means any full or part-time trade, profession or corporation.

. . . 9. **Insured** — means you and the following **persons** if permanent residents of your household
a. your relatives,
b. anyone under the age of 21,
Under Section II - Liability, **insured** also means:
c. any **person** or organization legally responsible for animals or watercraft owned by you, or anyone included in 9a or 9b, and covered by this policy. Any **person** or organization using or having custody of these animals or watercraft in the course of any **business** or without permission of the owner is not an **Insured**.
d. any **person** while employed by you or anyone in 9a or 9b with respect to any vehicle covered by this policy.

. . . 13. **Occurrence** means an accident including exposure to conditions which results during the policy period in **bodily injury** or **property damage**. Repeated or continuous exposure to the same general conditions is considered to be one **occurrence**.

. . . 15. **Property damage** — means physical injury to or destruction of tangible property covered by this policy and resulting loss of use.

Occurrence does not include accident or events which take place during the policy period which do not result in **bodily injury** or **property damage** until after the policy period.

SECTION II — LIABILITY
Coverages
Coverage E — Personal Liability

We will pay those damages which an **insured** becomes legally obligated to pay because of **bodily injury, property damage** or personal injury resulting from an **occurrence** to which this coverage applies . . .

SECTION II — EXCLUSIONS
Applying To Coverage E — Personal Liability

We do not cover:

2. Punitive or exemplary damages or the cost of defense related to such damages.

Applying to Coverage E and F - Personal Liability and Medical Payment to Others

We do not cover **bodily injury, property damage** or personal injury which:

> 1. arises from or during the course of **business** pursuits of an **insured**. . . .
> 3. is either:
>> a. caused intentionally by or at the direction of an **insured**; or
>> b. results from any **occurrence** caused by an intentional act of any **insured** where the results are reasonably foreseeable.

To recap the facts as we know them, you had just completed coaching an Arizona Cardinals game, and were on your way to the locker room. We believe that the Business Pursuits Exclusion would apply in this case. Additionally, it appears as though your actions would be considered intentional in nature. We, therefore, regretfully must inform you that we are unable to offer you defense and indemnification through your homeowners policy for claims arising out of this incident.

If you have any additional information you believe is relevant to this matter, please contact the undersigned or the claims representative assigned, Diane Griffith.

Very truly yours,

FARMERS INSURANCE COMPANY OF ARIZONA

Ken Sanders
Branch Claims Manager

KS:cj

cc: Les Zittrain, Attorney at Law

QUESTIONS

1. Does this letter put Farmers in breach of its duty to defend?
2. How does Farmers' approach differ from Gulf's approach? Is the difference one of different scopes of coverage (homeowner's versus employer's)? Or does the difference reflect dissimilar attitudes about risk tolerance? Note that at least one major issue, the intentionality of Joe's act, is important to both Gulf's and Farmers' coverage decisions.
3. How would you reply to the above letter from Farmers if you were Joe's attorney?

When Joe's personal attorney received the letter from Farmers, he pushed back. The following letter is Joe's attorney's response to Farmers' denial of coverage.

LAW OFFICES

ZITTRAIN AND ZITTRAIN

ATTORNEYS AT LAW

201 FRANKLIN PROFESSIONAL BUILDING
4240 GREENSBURG PIKE
PITTSBURGH, PA 15221-4235

LESTER E. ZITTRAIN*
RUTH A. ZITTRAIN**

*ALSO ADMITTED IN VIRGINIA
**ALSO ADMITTED IN FLORIDA

July 27, 2000

TELEPHONE
(412) 271-2200

FAX
(412) 271-2300

Certified Mail No. Z 328 279 395
Return Receipt Requested

Ken Sanders, Branch Claims Manager
Farmers Insurance Company of Arizona

               Re: **Insured:**
                       Policy No.:
                       Loss Date:
                       Claimant:
                       Claim No.:

Dear Mr. Sanders:

    I was indeed surprised to receive the copy of your July 20, 2000 letter addressed to Charles Greene regarding the captioned matter. In my opinion, the denial of a defense and indemnification to Mr. Greene by Farmers under its Protection Plus Homeowners Policy, particularly at this early stage of the proceedings, constitutes a breach by Farmers of its fiduciary obligation to its policyholder, Mr. Greene.

    In my previous conversations with Diane Griffith, she had indicated to me that Farmers would be issuing a Reservation of Rights letter to Mr. Greene; thus, my surprise at receiving your denial letter. Your reasoning for denial of coverage, again at this early stage, is flawed. The business pursuits ("course and scope") exclusion is by no means conclusive under the paucity of facts available to us. You, yourself, have stated that Mr. Greene had "...completed coaching an Arizona Cardinals football game."

    As to the "intentional act" exclusion, what was intended by Mr. Greene is a purely subjective matter involving an individual's state of mind and is subject to

ZITTRAIN AND ZITTRAIN

Ken Sanders
July 27, 2000
Page 2

resolution only after taking into consideration the totality of <u>all</u> the facts and circumstances in this particular setting.

Reading the language of the policy, in no event was the bodily injury caused intentionally. If Mr. Greene's striking of Mr. Cockriel was, under the circumstances, a reflex response or done as an act of self-defense, would that be interpreted as an intentional act under the policy? I doubt it. Furthermore, is a ruptured eardrum a reasonably foreseeable result of Mr. Greene's quest for self-preservation? Highly debatable.

In other words, your unilateral conclusion "...that the Business Pursuits Exclusion would apply in this case...." and "...it appears as though your actions would be considered intentional in nature...." are premature, not founded on the facts and circumstances available at this period in time, and are merely faulty avenues for Farmers to travel in wrongfully and in bad faith denying a defense to its premium paying policyholder.

I ask that you re-consider your position. If you insist on your position, then Mr. Greene will, under the appropriate circumstances, seriously consider negotiating a "Damron Agreement" with the plaintiff vis-à-vis compensatory damages and likewise a bad faith action against Farmers for punitive damages.

Very truly yours,

LESTER E. ZITTRAIN

LEZ:mme

cc: Mr. Charles E. Greene

What was Zittrain's motivation for writing this letter to Farmers, given that Joe had already been provided a defense by Gulf? First, there may be some reason to pursue the matter with Farmers considering that Gulf's provision of an attorney is not unconditional. Gulf reserved the right to withdraw from the defense should its obligation to defend terminate at any point during the suit. Getting Farmers to recognize a duty to defend might provide a back-up source of funding for Joe's defense. This is especially true should a court find that Joe was not engaging in a business pursuit at the time of the incident; that finding could excuse Gulf from having to defend or indemnify (since its insurance is limited to acts relating to the Cardinals) while simultaneously eliminating the "business pursuits" exception offered by Farmers as a reason why they should not have to defend.

A second reason to respond to Farmers' letter is to lay the groundwork for a possible "failure to defend" claim against the insurer. A failure to defend claim is a claim made by an insured against his insurance company alleging that the insurance company left him high and dry after he was sued — or otherwise failed to fulfill its duties to assist the insured. Should Joe later bring a claim against Farmers for failure to provide a defense, this letter will show that Farmers was aware of the ambiguities when it decided not to provide a defense.

Tort defendants who are compelled to settle (or simply lose) a suit because of a refusal by their insurance companies to defend could try to initiate a new suit against those companies under a theory of failure to defend. Of course, without good legal help, they might not even realize they have a cause of action, and the initial problem is that they are denied legal representation precisely when they needed it. The "Damron" agreement, mentioned in the last paragraph of Zittrain's letter above, is an obscure but important and controversial way around this problem. We return to the law and policy of Damron agreements later in this chapter.

Zittrain's response to Farmers' denial of coverage may have caused Farmers to further assess Joe's claim. The company sent a reply written by retained counsel rather than a claims adjuster.

LAW OFFICES

BROENING OBERG WOODS WILSON & CASS

PROFESSIONAL CORPORATION

August 3, 2000

Lester E. Zittrain
Zittrain and Zittrian
201 Franklin Professional Building
4240 Greensburg Pike
Pittsburgh, Pa 15221-4235

> *RE:*   *Insured:*
> *Policy No.:*
> *Claim No.:*
> *Date of Loss:*

Dear Mr. Zittrain:

I have been retained by the Farmers Insurance Company of Arizona with regard to your correspondence of July 27, 2000 as it relates to coverage for Charles Greene. I am in the process of gathering the information relating to this claim and of determining the current status of the litigation which I understand is being defended by the carrier for the Cardinals, Gulf Insurance. I assume that Mr. Greene is being defended in that action by Gulf, but if I am incorrect in this regard, please so advise.

Although I have not reached any final opinions or conclusions, I am in a position to briefly respond to some of the statements in your correspondence.

First of all, with regard to the business pursuits exclusion, Mr. Greene was still on the football field in Cardinals garb as part of an out of town football coaching trip and was returning to the locker room. The fact that the game had ended and he was not coaching at that particular moment does not in any way suggest that the bodily injury did not "arise from" the business pursuits of Mr. Greene.

Secondly, I have reviewed the videotape of the event. I invite you to do the same. Mr. Greene did not pull his foot back, attempt to push the vehicle off his foot, or take any other type of action which would appear to be reflex. What the tape reveals is that there was a brief exchange of words between Mr. Cockriel and Mr. Greene, after which Mr. Greene struck Cockriel in the side of the head.

In any event, as previously indicated, it is my understanding that litigation has been filed. I will review the allegations of the Complaint as well as any other available information and make recommendations to Farmers. I will get back to you as quickly as possible.

Very truly yours,

JAMES R BROENING
For the Firm

JRB/bzb

This letter from Farmers hews to the previous position of no coverage, but now the question sounds like an open one rather than one that has already been determined. However, on March 29, 2001 — six months after the letter above — Farmers reiterated its position that it would provide neither a defense nor indemnity.

The insurance carriers' decisions in these cases are not easy. If the insurer chooses to provide a defense and indemnify the defendant, the insurer may be required to pay for a large judgment and expensive legal work. On the other hand, if the carrier abandons the case, it faces the risk of being held liable for bad faith failure to defend and/or indemnify in a later action. Even if the insurer ultimately can prove it was right in refusing to defend, it may have to expend resources to defend itself against such a claim by the insured.

PART C: CONFLICTS

Once these initial coverage questions are exhausted, the insurance company may face a range of follow-on issues. In Joe's case, once Gulf had decided to offer a defense for him, it had to decide whether to appoint a single lawyer to represent both Joe and his employer, the Cardinals, who also were named defendants in the suit. The insurance company decided to provide separate attorneys because of the potential conflicts of interest between Joe and the Cardinals: Some facts might establish independent negligence by the Cardinals, which could be to Joe's advantage to emphasize, and Joe and his team might have different views about whether he was acting within the scope of his employment.

The Cardinals soon moved to be dismissed from the suit for reasons suggested in Chapters 3 and 4, and Joe's personal attorney wanted to go on the record when Joe's insurance company-appointed attorneys did not immediately move to oppose the dismissal:

LAW OFFICES

ZITTRAIN AND ZITTRAIN

ATTORNEYS AT LAW

201 FRANKLIN PROFESSIONAL BUILDING
4240 GREENSBURG PIKE
PITTSBURGH, PA 15221-4235

LESTER E. ZITTRAIN*
RUTH A. ZITTRAIN**

*ALSO ADMITTED IN VIRGINIA
**ALSO ADMITTED IN FLORIDA

July 31, 2001

TELEPHONE
(412) 271-2200

FAX
(412) 271-2300

Via FAX, Hard Copy to follow

William D. Holm, Esq.   Robert R. Berk, Esq.

Re: **Cockriel v. Arizona Cardinals,**
      Charles E. Greene, et al

Dear Bill and Bob:

Bob's letter of July 24, 2001 addressed to Joe Greene was received by me, as copy addressee, here in Pittsburgh on Friday, July 27. Apparently the original of the Cardinals' Motion for Summary Judgment was hand delivered to you on June 1, 2001 and the original of the Plaintiff's response thereto mailed to you on June 29, 2001. I would have been more comfortable had copies of these pleadings been provided to me without the delay involved.

In any event, I telephoned Bob on Friday because, as mentioned in his letter, I do "...have other thoughts..." with respect to your intention not to object or to otherwise take a position with regard to the Cardinals' Motion. I missed Bob who called back later that same day after I had left the office. I called again yesterday (Monday, July 30) and was informed that both of you were out of town.

It is clearly in our mutual client's (Joe!) best interests that the Cardinals' Motion be denied. To put it another way, it is clearly advantageous to Joe that the Cardinals remain as a party throughout the litigation.

I have digested the Motion for Summary Judgment which, frankly, would never pass muster here in Pennsylvania. The Cardinals assert they cannot be

---

Zittrain and Zittrain

William D. Holm, Esq.
Robert R. Berk, Esq.
July 31, 2001
Page 2

vicariously liable because Joe's slapping of the Plaintiff was *intentional* assuming that *intentional* automatically negates any respondeat superior responsibility on the part of the Cardinals. They also dwell on Joe's action as an *intentional* tort without any consideration of Joe's action being a "reflexive response" or an act of self-defense which a jury might very well interpret as nullifying any "intentional" aspect. This is covered and answered in the Plaintiff's response. Also, the "slapping by Joe not being within the course and scope of his employment" argument is clearly without merit and likewise addressed in the Plaintiff's response. There are a number of issues in the Cardinals-Greene relationship to be determined by the jury which ought to preclude dismissal of the Cardinals from the case at this time.

My professional career has been devoted essentially to the representation of plaintiffs in personal injury cases. I therefore called three different highly respected and competent defense lawyers from different defense firms here in Pittsburgh. I have dealt with all of them over the years in adversary situations. I did not speak with them out of any mistrust of lack of confidence in you. Far from it. If I differ from your present position vis-à-vis the Cardinals' Motion, I just wanted to make sure that my position was not strictly from a plaintiff's point of view and maybe off-the-wall. My colleagues assured me that this was not the case.

Without exception, they all agree that if they were representing Joe in this particular litigation under these particular circumstances, they would consider it imperative, as part of their duty to their client, to do whatever is legally possible to assure that the Cardinals are not dismissed from the suit, either preliminarily or at trial or thereafter. All defense counsel indicated to me that they, at this stage of the proceedings, would vigorously oppose the Cardinals' Motion for Summary Judgment.

Please call ASAP so we can discuss.

Sincerely,

LESTER E. ZITTRAIN

The reason that Joe's personal attorney was working so hard to ensure that Joe's insurance company-appointed attorneys oppose the Cardinals' motion to dismiss is that the impact of the Cardinals' being dismissed from the suit would be very damaging for Joe. If the Cardinals were dismissed, Joe would lose not only another defendant to absorb liability, but he also could lose the benefit of his insurance company-appointed attorneys' services.

Recall from the coverage letter sent to Joe by Gulf Insurance that the insurance was provided under a reservation of rights, and that Gulf retained the right to withdraw from Joe's defense if at any time "the potential for coverage no longer exists." If the Cardinals were dismissed from the suit on the grounds that Joe was not within the scope of his employment when the incident happened, that decision becomes the "law of the case." If Joe were not acting within the scope of his employment — a finding perhaps necessary to a decision to dismiss the Cardinals from the case — the Cardinals' insurance company would have no duty to provide a defense for Joe, even if Joe's conduct did not involve intentional harm. For Joe, the stakes in this decision were potentially very high.

Joe's insurance company-appointed attorneys did indeed oppose the Cardinals' motion to dismiss. The judge's ruling on the issue on summary judgment is reproduced below.

SUPERIOR COURT OF ARIZONA   *** FILED ***
MARICOPA COUNTY   09/28/2001

09/27/2001   CLERK OF THE COURT
                                          FORM V000A

JUDGE WILLIAM L. TOPF   A. Sandoval
                                          Deputy

CV 2000-010963

9:55 a.m.   Hearing concludes.

September 28, 2001

This matter has been under advisement.

Based on the record before the Court, the Court finds that even if the facts alleged in the Plaintiff's Complaint and Amended Complaint can be proved at trial, these facts do not give rise to a legal cause of action against the Defendants Arizona Cardinals, Inc. and B&B Holdings, Inc. The claims for vicarious liability against these two Defendants do not present any genuine issues of material fact. Specifically, the Plaintiff will not be able to prove at trial that the Defendant Greene was in the course and scope of his employment with the corporate Defendants, if he committed the acts that are alleged in the Complaint and Amended Complaint. The alleged conduct by Mr. Greene was not conduct that he was employed to perform and the alleged conduct would not have a purpose to benefit his employer. Moreover, the Plaintiff's claims in the Complaint and the Amended Complaint for general negligence or negligent hiring or supervision by the corporate Defendants cannot be proved at trial based on the pleadings and affidavits before the Court. The Plaintiff cannot meet the minimum standard under the Orme School test. A reasonable finder of fact could not conclude that the corporate Defendants were negligent under the factual allegations in this case.

Docket Code 019   Page 2

```
              SUPERIOR COURT OF ARIZONA        *** FILED ***
                   MARICOPA COUNTY             09/28/2001

09/27/2001                                CLERK OF THE COURT
                                               FORM V000A

JUDGE WILLIAM L. TOPF                        A. Sandoval
                                             Deputy

CV 2000-010963
```

Therefore, the Court finds that there are no genuine issues of material fact on any of the claims in the Complaint or the proposed Amended Complaint against the corporate Defendants and that the corporate Defendants are entitled to a summary judgment as a matter of law.

IT IS ORDERED granting the corporate Defendants' Motion for Summary Judgment.

IT IS FURTHER ORDERED that judgment shall be granted in favor of the Defendants Arizona Cardinals, Inc. and B&B Holdings, Inc. and against the Plaintiff on all the Plaintiff's claims in the Complaint and the Amended Complaint against these Defendants. The Plaintiff shall take nothing on his claims against these Defendants.

The *Orme School* test cited in the judge's opinion is not a case about scope of employment; rather, it simply sets forth a standard in Arizona for when summary judgment is appropriate. The court's standard there should look vaguely familiar to those who have seen Rule 56 of the Federal Rules of Civil Procedure; *Orme School* held that when evaluating motions for summary judgment, "Either motion should be granted if the facts produced in support of the claim or defense have so little probative value, given the quantum of evidence required, that reasonable people could not agree with the conclusion advanced by the proponent of the claim or defense." Orme School v. Reeves, 802 P.2d 1000, 1008 (Ariz. 1990).

The court here apparently believed that even construing the facts as favorably as possible to the plaintiff — and therefore as parsimoniously as possible to the Cardinals — it was still impossible for a reasonable juror to conclude that the Cardinals bore any liability for the incident, whether on an independent theory of negligence (see Chapter 3), or because the prerequisites were met for vicarious liability (see Chapter 4). Trial courts rule on dozens of motions in relatively rapid succession; the lengthy, self-conscious opinions excerpted in law school casebooks are by no means representative of a typical memorandum of law issued by a trial judge — such memoranda can leave much of the reasoning to the imagination of the reader.

QUESTIONS

1. What is the basis cited by the judge for dismissing the Cardinals from the suit?
2. How might this decision affect the duty of the Cardinals' insurance company, Gulf, to provide a defense for Joe?
3. How might this decision affect Joe's argument that his homeowners' insurance provider, Farmers, is obligated to provide a defense for him?

Joe's insurance company-appointed attorneys faced a new question once the Cardinals were dismissed from the suit. Because it is not clear that the Cardinals' insurance company was required to continue providing a defense for Joe once the judge found that the Cardinals were not liable in the suit, the insurance attorneys appointed to represent Joe then faced a tough choice — they were paid by the insurance company, and the insurance company could benefit by discontinuing coverage for Joe. However, as Joe's lawyers, they knew that Joe would benefit from continued representation.

The lawyers decided to send the Cardinals' insurance carrier a simple notice of the court's dismissal of the Cardinals from the suit without further comment, and await a response from the insurance carrier. The insurance carrier never acted to discontinue Joe's defense.

QUESTION

After reviewing Gulf's original letter offering its rationale for defending under a reservation of rights, can you think of any way to read the judge's opinion that leaves open the possibility that Gulf still owed a duty to defend Joe?

PART D: ENDGAME: PLAINTIFF AND DEFENDANT TEAM UP

So far as the narrative of Parts A and B in this chapter has progressed, Joe has an attorney (provided for him by Gulf, his employer's insurance company), and the employer — the Cardinals — is out of the suit. This combination of factors does not bode well for the plaintiff, who has lost the Cardinals' deep pockets, yet is left with a defendant (Joe) who is not paying for his own defense, and therefore has little interest in cutting short the defense in order to settle. The situation is not optimal for Joe, either. Joe is now the only defendant in the suit; there is no one left to share the blame. Joe has an insurance company-appointed defense attorney, but that attorney's continued assistance is in jeopardy because of the Cardinals' dismissal. Moreover, Joe has no good reason to believe that the insurance company will indemnify him if a judgment goes against him in the suit.

Joe's interests align with Mark's in one respect — unless Mark is bringing the case to truly hit Joe where it hurts, they both hope that any judgment will be covered by Joe's (or the Cardinals') insurance provider. For Mark, this is a far easier means of collection on a judgment than seeking a sheriff's sale to liquidate Joe's property to satisfy the judgment, or expecting that Joe simply has thousands of dollars available in a bank account.

Mark and Joe's interest in involving an insurance company in the case aligns with the public policy of most states favoring a rule that requires insurance companies to provide a defense except in cases in which the lack of coverage is very clear. It can be difficult to monitor insurance companies' decisions regarding whether to provide a defense to their insureds. If there is little danger of recourse, it will always be in the insurance company's interest to deny provision of a defense, because defending is often expensive. An insured defendant whose insurance company refuses to provide a defense often has very few resources to devote to a suit against his insurance company during or after the time he is sued by a tort plaintiff. If that's the case, simply giving the insured a contract claim against his insurance company for inappropriately failing to defend him — perhaps hoping that the erstwhile defendant can find a contingency-fee-accepting plaintiff's lawyer to help sue the insurance company — may not be an effective method of policing the contract. Administrative regulation of insurance companies — through which defendants displeased with their coverage can file a complaint for later investigation — has its own important limitations. To increase the stakes for insurance companies making decisions about whether to provide a defense to an insured defendant, some states allow the following kind of agreement between a tort plaintiff and tort defendant.

A "Damron" Agreement Against an Insurance Company That Has Failed to Defend

1. **Resolution of the Case Between Tort Plaintiff and Tort Defendant:** First, the defendant agrees to stop fighting the plaintiff's claim of liability. This may mean failing to appeal an adverse judgment from trial, or stipulating to one's liability before, during, or after trial, and having a judge formally enter judgment on that stipulation. In some cases there is no judgment, but merely a settlement agreement between the plaintiff and defendant. Obviously, this part of the agreement helps the plaintiff.

2. **Covenant Not to Execute Against the Defendant:** The plaintiff, now with judgment or settlement agreement in hand, agrees not to execute the judgment or agreement against the defendant personally. In other words, the defendant will not have to pay the settlement/judgment against him. This part of the agreement is a relief to the defendant, and without step 3 seems to make the deal a complete loser for the plaintiff — step 1 is rendered a Pyrrhic victory.

3. **Assignment of Defendant's Claim Against the Defendant's Insurance Company to Plaintiff:** As we have seen, a defendant whose insurance company has refused to provide a defense for him in a suit has a potential claim against the insurance company for bad faith failure to defend. In a Damron agreement, the defendant assigns that claim to the plaintiff. The plaintiff, standing in the shoes of the defendant, then sues the defendant's insurance company to collect on the judgment or settlement from the tort suit. The defendant is now effectively insulated from any financial liability — even though he stipulated to the truth of the plaintiff's claims — and the plaintiff can try to sue the defendant's insurance company under the original (or, for that matter, an amended) theory of the case. The former defendant is now merely a bystander to the new suit — even though the insurance company's liability in that suit will in large part depend on the nature of the first suit, which could call for testimony from the original, now financially disinterested, defendant.

The Damron agreement evolved from the creative minds of attorneys faced with the problem of insurance companies refusing to defend and/or indemnify insured defendants, leaving both the plaintiff and defendant in a bad position. This text refers to these agreements as Damron agreements after a case — you can guess the title — that validated the use of this type of agreement in Arizona.[2] Because Mark's suit against Joe took place in Arizona, the parties also refer to the agreement as a "Damron" agreement. Similar agreements are called by different names, and governed by different rules, in other states.[3] Not all states welcome them. Since state legal codes are typically silent on their propriety, state supreme courts consider the validity of these agreements without guidance from their legislatures, as cases come up in which such agreements are implicated. In *Red Giant Oil Co v. Lawlor*, excerpted below, the Iowa Supreme Court accepts the validity of a Damron-like agreement, considering and rejecting in turn some of the powerful arguments *against* countenancing such agreements.

RED GIANT OIL COMPANY v. LAWLOR
528 N.W. 2d 524 (1995)

IV.   THE MERITS

For reasons that follow, we are more convinced by the line of authority permitting the settlement agreements in question than we are with the line of authority that does not. As we mentioned earlier, one of the leading cases approving of such agreements is *Metcalf.*

Because the facts in *Metcalf* are somewhat similar to the facts here, we recite them. In an underlying tort suit, a party injured in a collision sued an insured under a policy on the other car involved. The insurer disavowed coverage and refused to defend the insured. During the course of trial, the parties settled. As part of the settlement the insured consented to an entry of judgment against him for $4500 and costs. The injured party agreed not to attempt collection from any assets of the insured other than insurance policies that covered the insured. Following entry of judgment, the injured party garnished the insurer on the judgment. The insurer defended on two grounds. First, the insurer claimed there was no coverage. Second, the policy obligated the insurer to pay "all sums which the insured shall become legally obligated to pay as damages." The judgment and the agreement — the insurer argued — created no obligation to pay on the part of the insured and, therefore, no obligation on the part of the insurer to pay. *Metcalf,* 176 Neb. at 474, 126 N.W.2d at 475.

The trial court found against the insurer on both issues. The appellate court agreed. As to the second defense, the appellate court concluded that the judgment in the

---

[2] *See* Damron v. Sledge, 460 P.2d 997 (Ariz. 1969).
[3] A survey of such agreements can be found in Justin A. Harris, *Judicial Approaches to Stipulated Judgments, Assignments of Rights, and Covenants Not to Execute in Insurance Litigation* (Note), 47 Drake L. Rev. 853, nn.22, 23, 30, and 31 (1999).

underlying tort action created a legal liability within the meaning of the policy. In reaching this conclusion, the court said:

> The [insurer] is obligated under its insurance policy to defend the suit brought against [the insured].... This it refused to do. [The insured] was thereupon required to engage an attorney and provide his own defense. With the insurance company denying liability, [the insured] was entitled to use all reasonable means of avoiding personal liability. It was to [the insured's] personal interest to consent to the $4500 judgment and accept an agreement from the [injured party] not to execute on [the insured's] property other than any rights to indemnity he might have in the designated insurance policies. The matter is of no consequence to [the insurer] if its claim of nonliability is correct. Since its claim of nonliability has no validity, and it having declined to defend the action when called upon to do so, the [insurer] is in no position to attack the judgment in the absence of fraud, collusion, or bad faith. If the judgment was obtained in good faith, the [insurer] may not again litigate the issues that resulted in the judgment.

Metcalf, 176 Neb. at 475, 126 N.W.2d at 475-76....

Having resolved the policy language defense against the insurer, the *Metcalf* court proceeded to decide the case on the basis of a well-settled indemnity rule. The rule provides that, in the absence of fraud or collusion, an insurance company that refuses to defend its insured is bound by a judgment against the insured with respect to all matters which were litigated or could have been litigated in that action. *Paynter,* 122 Ariz. at 200, 593 P.2d at 950; see also Jones v. Southern Sur. Co., 210 Iowa 61, 69, 230 N.W. 381, 385 (1929). This rule is based upon

> the broad duty of the insurer to defend claims under policy provisions [in which the insurer agrees to defend the insured]. Under such [language], the insured is entitled to a defense in any case in which there is coverage under the policy. "A purchaser of liability insurance has a right to expect not only indemnification at the end but also a shield against liability claims at the outset." By refusing to defend, the insurer takes the risk that it may have erred in determining that the policy did not provide coverage. Having refused to provide a defense, the insurer is said to have been "vouched in" the action against the insured and is bound by the judgment. In the absence of fraud or collusion, it is not entitled to relitigate the merits of the claim.

Paynter, 122 Ariz. at 200, 593 P.2d at 950-51 (citations omitted)....

In face of this indemnity rule, an insurer has two options when it is asked to defend an action against its insured. It can defend with notice to the insured that it is reserving the right to challenge its liability on the policy. Or, it can repudiate liability, refuse to defend, and take its chances. Elliot v. Casualty Ass'n of Am., 254 Mich. 282, 285, 236 N.W. 782, 783 (1931). If it chooses the latter option, then in the absence of fraud or collusion, *Elliot* holds that the insurer should be bound by the judgment. *Id.* at 285, 236 N.W. at 783....

Second, we think the *Metcalf* rationale which is based on *Fullerton* — an Iowa case — provides an additional reason to hold that a stipulated judgment and covenant not to execute do not invalidate coverage. As we said, that rationale simply means that an insurer may not hide behind policy language after it abandons its insured and the insured settles the claim by such an agreement.

Third, we agree with those courts which hold that a claim by an insured against the insurer for failure of the insurer to defend may be assigned to the injured party. Prejudgment assignments — like the one here — in return for covenants not to execute are not inherently collusive or fraudulent. Damron v. Sledge, 105 Ariz. 151, 153, 460 P.2d 997, 999 (1969); *Critz,* 230 Cal. App. 2d at 802, 41 Cal. Rptr. at 409. Such agreements are consistent with the general rule of indemnity that permits insureds to protect themselves against insurers who wrongfully refuse to defend.

An assignment is a transfer to another of the whole of any property or right in the property. Broyles v. Iowa Dep't of Social Servs., 305 N.W.2d 718, 721 (Iowa 1981) (citation omitted). In such transfers, the assignee assumes the rights, remedies and benefits of the assignor. *Id.* at 723 (citation omitted). On the other hand, the assignee also takes the property subject to all defenses to which the assignor is subject. Van Maanen v. Van Maanen, 360 N.W.2d 758, 762 (Iowa 1985); Iowa Code § 539.1. Choses in action whether for breach of contract or for tort are assignable in this state. Fischer v. Klink, 234 Iowa 884, 888, 14 N.W.2d 695, 698 (1944). In light of these rules and because insurers have available to them a variety of defenses — for example, coverage, fraud, and collusion — we fail to see why legally it should make any difference who sues the insurer — the insured or the insured's assignee. . . .

Fourth, we see nothing in settlement agreements like the one here that would tend to be injurious to the public or contrary to the public good. . . .

We agree with Red Giant that implicit in the *Freeman* and Iowa district court holdings is a policy determination. That policy determination is that it is better to allow an insurer to breach its duty to an insured and escape liability than to risk occasional fraud or collusion. We think such a policy determination would render meaningless the rule of indemnity in wrongful refusal to defend cases and ignores the law of assignment.

Last, the fear that fraud or collusion is possible should not be the test. We rejected a similar argument in disposing of interspousal immunity, noting that our system of justice "is adequately equipped to discern the existence of fraud and collusion." Shook v. Crabb, 281 N.W.2d 616, 620 (Iowa 1979).

When the insurer has wrongfully refused to defend and the insured reaches a settlement with the injured party, most courts have held that a settlement is presumptive evidence of the liability of the insured and the amount of damages. In addition, the insurer has the burden of rebutting this presumption by showing the settlement was procured as a result of fraud or collusion. Griggs v. Bertram, 88 N.J. 347, 362, 443 A.2d 163, 172 (1982) (citing the jurisdictions following the rule). Indeed, this court long ago embraced this rule. *Jones,* 210 Iowa at 69, 230 N.W. at 385. As *Griggs* points out, "[t]his rule is consistent with the general assumption that in the absence of contrary evidence, persons act fairly, honestly, and in good faith." *Griggs,* 88 N.J. at 364, 443 A.2d at 172.

But here the judgment is not an adjudication on the merits. It is only the settlement Red Giant and Coyle reached. There was no real trial. So in these circumstances, while the judgment is binding and valid as to Coyle and Red Giant, it is not conclusive as to LeMars, the insurer. See Miller v. Shugart, 316 N.W.2d 729, 735 (Minn. 1982) (reaching the same conclusion as to settlement reached under circumstances similar to those here).

A535 In these circumstances we think the indemnity rule applicable where insurers wrongfully refuse to defend should be modified as the court did in *Miller.* Following this indemnity rule, the court imposed the burden of persuasion on the insurer to prove a stipulated judgment between the insured and the injured party was reached through fraud or collusion and therefore unenforceable against the insurer. *Miller,* 316 N.W.2d at 734. The insurer in *Miller* never pled fraud nor collusion. Nor did the insurer submit affidavits in opposition to the injured party's motion for summary judgment or other evidence to make out any fact issue of fraud or collusion. So the court found as a matter of law that the judgment was not obtained by fraud or collusion. *Id.*

But the inquiry did not end there. The court went one step further and required a showing that the settlement on which the judgment was based was reasonable and prudent. *Id.* at 734-35. As to this issue, the court imposed the burden of persuasion on the injured party. In doing so, the court adopted an objective test: "what a reasonably prudent person in the position of the defendant would have settled for on the merits of the plaintiff's claim." *Id.* at 735. This test — the court explained — "involves a consideration of the facts bearing on the liability and damage aspects of plaintiff's claim, as well as the risks of going to trial." *Id.; see also* Wolff v. Royal Ins. Co., 472 N.W.2d 233, 235 (S.D. 1991) (citation omitted) . . .

We hold therefore that in settlements like the one here, an insurer, relying on fraud or collusion, must plead and prove these defenses. If either defense is proven, the settlement is invalid and unenforceable against the insurer. The injured party, however, has the burden to prove by a preponderance of the evidence that (1) the underlying claim was covered by the policy, and (2) the settlement which resulted in the judgment was reasonable and prudent. The test the fact finder must apply on this issue is what a reasonable and prudent person in the position of the defendant (Coyle) would have paid to settle the plaintiff's (Red Giant's) claim. In applying this test, the fact finder must consider facts bearing on the liability and damage aspects of the claim as well as the risks of going to trial. . . .

Because of the conclusions we reach, we must reverse and remand for further proceedings consistent with this opinion.

REVERSED AND REMANDED.

QUESTIONS

1. Since the plaintiff in a Damron agreement promises by contract never to collect from the defendant the sum that the defendant agrees he owes under the plaintiff's claims, is it credible to assert that the money is really owed to the plaintiff by the defendant's insurance company if it wrongly failed to defend? In what way did the defendant ever really owe the money to the plaintiff?

2. Do Damron agreements make sense? How do they compare to alternatives that might exist to keep insurance companies in line?

Recall that Joe's homeowner's insurance carrier (Farmers) refused to cover the claim altogether (*i.e.,* refused both to defend and to indemnify Joe), and that Joe's employer's insurance carrier (Gulf) provided a defense but reserved the right not to indemnify Joe. Mark's suit against Joe never reached trial, because Mark and Joe made a "Damron" agreement similar to that discussed in the case above. The following documents from the case show the agreement between Mark and Joe that led ultimately to Mark's suit against Farmers. Had he chosen to do so, Mark also could have sued Gulf — the Cardinals' insurance carrier — for failing to accept a reasonable settlement offer. The correspondence reproduced below shows the parties coming to terms on the Damron agreement.

In the letter reproduced below, Joe's insurance company-appointed attorney negotiates the terms of a potential Damron agreement with the plaintiff's attorney.

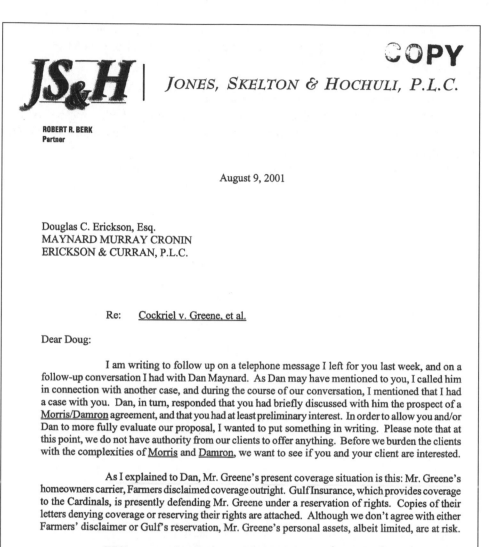

JS&H | JONES, SKELTON & HOCHULI, P.L.C.

ROBERT R. BERK
Partner

August 9, 2001

Douglas C. Erickson, Esq.
MAYNARD MURRAY CRONIN
ERICKSON & CURRAN, P.L.C.

           Re: <u>Cockriel v. Greene, et al.</u>

Dear Doug:

          I am writing to follow up on a telephone message I left for you last week, and on a follow-up conversation I had with Dan Maynard. As Dan may have mentioned to you, I called him in connection with another case, and during the course of our conversation, I mentioned that I had a case with you. Dan, in turn, responded that you had briefly discussed with him the prospect of a <u>Morris/Damron</u> agreement, and that you had at least preliminary interest. In order to allow you and/or Dan to more fully evaluate our proposal, I wanted to put something in writing. Please note that at this point, we do not have authority from our clients to offer anything. Before we burden the clients with the complexities of <u>Morris</u> and <u>Damron</u>, we want to see if you and your client are interested.

          As I explained to Dan, Mr. Greene's present coverage situation is this: Mr. Greene's homeowners carrier, Farmers disclaimed coverage outright. Gulf Insurance, which provides coverage to the Cardinals, is presently defending Mr. Greene under a reservation of rights. Copies of their letters denying coverage or reserving their rights are attached. Although we don't agree with either Farmers' disclaimer or Gulf's reservation, Mr. Greene's personal assets, albeit limited, are at risk.

          With one exception, the terms of the Morris/Damron[1] agreement would be dictated by your client. The one exception is that the agreement would have to include your client's covenant not to seek collection from Mr. Greene or his wife. Typically, Morris/Damron agreements include a stipulation regarding liability, a stipulated damage amount and an assignment to the plaintiff of the defendant's rights against his or her carrier(s), and a covenant not to execute against the insureds' personal assets, except for the insurance policies. In the present case, should we reach an agreement,

---

    [1] The reason that we refer to the potential agreement as a "Morris/Damron" agreement is that Morris agreements are used when there is a reservation of rights, while Damron agreements are used when there is a complete rejection of coverage. Given that the present case presents both situations, both Morris and Damron are implicated.

JONES, SKELTON & HOCHULI, P.L.C.

August 9, 2001
Page 2

Mr. and Mrs. Greene would assign their rights against both Farmers and Gulf. As I am sure you understand, however, the covenant with regard to Mr. and Mrs. Greene would not be contingent upon your client's success on the coverage issues. Put another way, the agreement would completely and without limitation insulate the Greenes from any Judgment(s) entered against them.

While we obviously cannot make any promises about what your client might recover from Farmers or Gulf, we believe that the agreement holds some obvious advantages for Mr. Cockriel. First, while we do not want to argue the merits here, we believe we have an excellent chance at a defense verdict. Given that your client ran over Mr. Greene's foot, and that Mr. Greene struck your client immediately thereafter, there is a distinct possibility, in our opinion, that the jury will conclude that both parties were at fault and that no one should recover anything. In other words, a "plague in both houses". Obviously, a stipulation as to liability eliminates this possibility, and similarly eliminates the possibility that a jury will find Mr. Cockriel comparatively negligent. Second, even if the jury decides to award damages to Mr. Cockriel, there is a reasonable likelihood, given his limited medical expenses, that the award will be nominal. Again, a stipulated judgment amount (or ex-parte damages hearing) would eliminate that possibility. Finally, as we believe you are aware, Mr. Greene has limited assets and would be unable to satisfy any significant judgment. As a result, your client is probably going to have to look to Mr. Greene's insurance carriers in any event. Given that fact, Mr. Cockriel might want to avail himself of the potential advantages associated with a Morris/Damron agreement.

In addition to stipulating to liability and damages, Mr. Greene would be willing to stipulate to amend the Complaint to add a claim for negligence if you conclude that such a claim is appropriate under the facts as they have been developed through discovery. A negligence claim might enhance the coverage claims against the carriers. Again, however, the terms of the Morris/Damron would be up to you, provided Mr. and Mrs. Greene receive the unconditional covenant discussed above. We are not particularly concerned how the agreement is structured.

I want to again emphasize that we are not making an offer at this time, and that we do not have authority from, nor have we even discussed the possibility of a Morris/Damron agreement with our clients. We do not want to waste our time explaining the complexities of such an agreement to our clients if you have no interest. After you have had a chance to discuss this issue with your client, please give me a call.

Very truly yours,

Robert R. Berk
For the Firm

RRB/jh
Enclosures

Joe's attorney essentially gives to the plaintiff the ability to dictate the terms of the agreement, in return for the plaintiff's releasing Joe from personal liability on the judgment. There are two interesting upshots of this counterintuitive proposed end to the suit. First, this agreement means that the plaintiff will be able to choose the dollar amount of the stipulated judgment. Once the plaintiff stipulates judgment, he may be able to use that judgment as evidence of damages in the bad faith action against the insurance company. Consider whether there are policy concerns that arise from a plaintiff's being able to determine the amount of the judgment — and how the Iowa court in the *Red Giant* case above may have anticipated this problem and dealt with it.

Second, this agreement has the theoretically adversarial plaintiff and defendant coming together against the defendant's insurance company. If the agreement goes through, Mark has let Joe out of the suit, agreeing not to make Joe personally pay *any* money, in order to bring suit for a potentially large award against Joe's insurance company. If the point of the suit for Mark was outrage about Joe's conduct, why would Mark choose to enter this agreement? Similarly, if Joe regarded this as an offensive nuisance suit by Mark, why would Joe make an agreement with Mark that allows Mark to keep the suit alive against Joe's insurers?

The attorneys involved did manage to forge — but not yet sign — an agreement, and Joe's attorney wrote him the following letter to explain what he could now expect.

LAW OFFICES

Zittrain and Zittrain

ATTORNEYS AT LAW

201 FRANKLIN PROFESSIONAL BUILDING

4240 GREENSBURG PIKE

PITTSBURGH, PA 15221-4235

LESTER E. ZITTRAIN*
RUTH A. ZITTRAIN**

*ALSO ADMITTED IN VIRGINIA
**ALSO ADMITTED IN FLORIDA

TELEPHONE
(412) 271-2200

FAX
(412) 271-2300

November 9, 2001

Mr. Charles E. Greene
3380 S. Horizon Place
Chandler, AZ 85248

Dear Joe:

Just an update on a couple of things.

Only today have I finalized with Arizona counsel the Morris/Damron agreement regarding the Cockriel litigation. The following should now occur:

1.   Plaintiff's counsel will give notice to the insurance company that the agreement will be signed if the company still insists on its "reservation of rights" with respect to defending and indemnifying you (as to Gulf Insurance Co.);

2.   Notice will probably not be given to Farmers Insurance Co. (your homeowner's policy) because Farmers completely denied and rejected coverage from day one and thus Farmers is not entitled to notice;

3.   It is a 99.99% sure bet that Gulf will not "take the bait";

4.   When that happens, you and the plaintiff will then sign the agreement, as a result of which:

(a)   judgment will be entered for $100,000.00 against you alone;

(b)   plaintiff agrees that he will not now or ever execute or come after you or Agnes to satisfy the judgment;

(c)   all claims against Agnes and the Cardinals will be dismissed by order of court;

Once the parties agreed to pursue a Damron agreement, Joe's insurance company-appointed attorney faced the unenviable task of notifying his employer, Gulf insurance, that his client, Joe, had entered an agreement that threatened Gulf (in addition to Farmers) with a direct claims by the plaintiff. This is because Gulf defended only under a reservation of rights. The letter appears below.

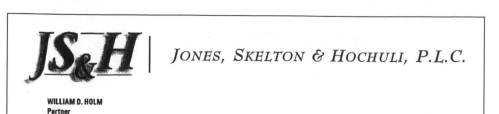

WILLIAM D. HOLM
Partner

November 26, 2001

Sent Via Fax and U.S. Mail

Larry Watkins
GULF INSURANCE

Re: Claim #   :
        Insured   :
        Claimant   :
        D/Loss   :

Dear Mr. Watkins:

The purpose of this letter is to report that the Greenes are planning to enter into a Settlement Agreement with the Plaintiffs to protect their personal and business assets, except for insurance policies, unless Gulf agrees to unconditionally defend and indemnify the Greenes pursuant to the terms and conditions of their insurance policy. As you know, Gulf is currently defending this lawsuit under a reservation of rights. Because Gulf may later decide there is no coverage for the claims brought by the Plaintiff, the Greenes have tentatively agreed to enter into a <u>Morris v. USAA</u> type Settlement Agreement with the Plaintiff.

Should Gulf withdraw the reservation of rights and agree to unconditionally defend and indemnify the Greenes for any liability or judgment that might be entered against them, the parties will not execute the attached <u>Morris</u> type Settlement Agreement. Under the <u>Morris</u> case, the parties are required to give the insurer reasonable notice of the proposed agreement and an opportunity to revisit their decision concerning coverage before finalizing any settlement. Thus, if Gulf maintains its current position and does not rescind the pending reservation of rights within one (1) week from the date of this letter, the parties will execute the attached Settlement Agreement.

JONES, SKELTON & HOCHULI, P.L.C.

November 26, 2001
Page 2 _____

Should you have any questions, please feel free to give me a call.

Sincerely,

William D. Holm
For the Firm

WDH:srs
cc: Les Zittrain
    Edward & Agnes Greene
    Douglas Erickson

Note that this letter is being sent to Gulf by an attorney that Gulf is paying for — telling Gulf that a deal has been worked out that could possibly put Gulf on the hook for the amount of the stipulated judgment.

As predicted, after exploring the prospect of a small settlement with Mark, Gulf refused to withdraw its reservation of right, and the agreement was signed. As the correspondence indicates, Farmers was not told anything further about the prospect of a Damron agreement beyond the prospect raised in the July 2000 letter sent to Farmers protesting its first refusal to provide a defense, reproduced on pp. 128–29.

Why would the parties want to avoid renewing notice to Farmers of their planned Damron agreement? As a strategic matter, perhaps the parties are not providing notice to Farmers because *both* parties would prefer to have Farmers continue to refuse to defend at this point, so that the settlement agreement will work. If the purpose of the Damron agreement is to police the provision of defense to insureds by insurance companies, then arguably they should give notice to Farmers in order to prod Farmers into providing a defense. On the other hand, if Farmers only agrees to provide a defense this late in the litigation process, perhaps providing notification and allowing Farmers an "out" now would destroy the policing aspects of the Damron agreement.

Below are the settlement agreement and stipulated judgment that together comprise a Damron agreement between Mark and Joe, found on file with the court.

SETTLEMENT AGREEMENT

Mark Cockriel v. Arizona Cardinals, et al.

Cause No. CV 2000-010963

RECITALS

1.   Mark Cockriel ("Plaintiff") is the Plaintiff in Cause No. CV2000-010963 (the "lawsuit") which is now pending in the Superior Court of the State of Arizona, County of Maricopa. The Defendants in the lawsuit are Charles Edward Greene a/k/a Mean Joe Greene and Agnes Greene, husband and wife ("Defendants Greene"), Arizona Cardinals, Inc. and B&B Holdings, Inc.

2.   In the lawsuit, Plaintiff seeks to recover damages from Defendants in connection with an "incident" that occurred on or about October 31, 1999.

3.   At the time of the incident, Defendants Greene were insured under a policy (#88 91539 80 45) issued by Farmers Insurance Company of Arizona ("Farmers").

4.   By letter dated July 20, 2000 (attached as Exhibit A), Farmers disclaimed and/or denied coverage for the incident.

5.   At the time of the incident, Defendants B&B Holdings, Inc., d/b/a Arizona Cardinals were insured under a policy (#03-00028-57-52) issued by Select Insurance Company ("Select"), a member of the Gulf Insurance Group ("Gulf").

6.   By letter dated May 24, 2000 (attached as Exhibit B) Select reserved its rights regarding its obligation to defend and indemnify Defendants Greene in connection with the incident.

1

7.   Plaintiff, Defendants Greene and their respective counsel have considered the facts and law, have analyzed the litigation which is pending between the parties and have concluded that it is in the best interest of each party herein to resolve any uncertainty in the pending litigation without any further delay.

COVENANTS:

1.   Plaintiff and Defendant Charles Edward Greene hereby agree to stipulate to a judgment ("Stipulated Judgment") in the amount of $100,000, in favor of Plaintiff and against Charles Edward Greene on Count Five of the Amended Complaint in the lawsuit. An approved form of the Stipulation for Entry of Judgment is attached as Exhibit C and an approved form of the Stipulated Judgment is attached as Exhibit D.

2.   The parties agree that the amount of the Stipulated Judgment is fair and reasonable under all of the circumstances.

3.   Plaintiff agrees to dismiss, with prejudice, all claims against Defendant Charles Edward Greene other than those set forth in Count Five of the Amended Complaint, and further agrees to dismiss, with prejudice, his claims against all other Defendants in the lawsuit. A copy of the Stipulation for Dismissal With Prejudice as to all other Defendants is attached as Exhibit E.

4.   As a material inducement for Plaintiff to enter into this Settlement Agreement, Defendant Charles Edward Greene agrees as follows:

A.   Defendant Charles Edward Greene shall reasonably cooperate with Plaintiff in all future proceedings against Farmers, Select or Gulf which relate to the incident.

2

B.   Defendant Charles Edward Greene will not knowingly take any position or give testimony that is materially inconsistent with his prior testimony in the lawsuit.

5.   Defendant Charles Edward Greene, for valuable consideration, hereby assigns to Plaintiff any and all claims, including bad faith claims, Defendant Charles Edward Greene has or may have against Farmers, Select or Gulf, which relate to the incident.

6.   Plaintiff covenants and agrees that he, his heirs and assigns, agents and/or attorneys will not execute against the personal, individual, business or community assets or holdings of any of Defendants Greene or any other Defendants in the lawsuit, or on any Judgment that is obtained in the lawsuit. Instead, Plaintiff covenants and agrees that he shall execute solely against Farmers, Select and/or Gulf on any Judgment entered in this case. The parties further acknowledge, agree and understand that Plaintiff's covenant and agreement not to execute against Defendants' assets is valid and enforceable whether or not Plaintiff is successful in collecting any additional monies from Farmers, Select, Gulf or anyone else.

7.   The parties further agree that the existence and terms of this Agreement, and of the Stipulated Judgment , shall be confidential, and that they shall not disclose to any third person said confidential information except as may be necessary in connection with Plaintiff's collection efforts against Farmers, Select or Gulf.

8.   The parties further agree that the provisions of this Settlement Agreement shall be binding upon the heirs, executors, administrators and assigns of the undersigned parties.

3

9.　　By signing below the parties intend to be legally bound hereby and represent that all provisions of this Settlement Agreement are true and correct to the best of their information and belief.

Plaintiff　　　　　　　　　　　　　　　　**Defendant**

---------------------------------　　　　　　　---------------------------------
MARK COCKRIEL　　　　　　　　　　CHARLES EDWARD GREENE

STATE OF ARIZONA　　　)
　　　　　　　　　　　　　　　)ss.
County of Maricopa　　　　　)

On this _28_ day of _November_, 2001, before me, the undersigned Notary Public, personally appeared Mark Cockriel, known to me as the person whose name is subscribed to the foregoing instrument, and acknowledged to me that he executed the same for the purposes therein contained.

　　　IN WITNESS WHEREOF, I hereunto set my hand and official seal.

My Commission Expires:　　　　　　　　　　　　　Notary Public

OFFICIAL SEAL
SHERRY A. HARE
Notary Public - State of Arizona
MARICOPA COUNTY
My Comm. Expires Oct. 20, 2002

STATE OF ARIZONA　　　)
　　　　　　　　　　　　　　　)ss.
County of Maricopa　　　　　)

On this _10_ day of _December_, 2001, before me, the undersigned Notary Public, personally appeared Charles Edward Greene, known to me as the person whose name is subscribed to the foregoing instrument, and acknowledged to me that he executed the same for the purposes therein contained.

　　　IN WITNESS WHEREOF, I hereunto set my hand and official seal.

　　　　　　　　　　　　　　　　　　　　　　Notary Public

My Commission Expires:

OFFICIAL SEAL
JUDY L. MALONEY
NOTARY PUBLIC-ARIZONA
MARICOPA COUNTY
My Comm. Expires Oct. 1, 2005

4

The foregoing Assignment is approved this **28th** day of **November**, 2001, by Douglas C. Erickson of MAYNARD MURRAY CRONIN ERICKSON & CURRAN, P.L.C., attorneys for Plaintiff.

> MAYNARD MURRAY CRONIN
> ERICKSON & CURRAN, P.L.C.
>
>
> By: _____
> Douglas C. Erickson
> Suite 1800
> 3200 North Central Avenue
> Phoenix, Arizona 85012
> Attorneys for Plaintiff

The foregoing Assignment is approved this _10^t_ day of _December_, 2001, by Robert R. Berk of JONES, SKELTON and HOCHULI, P.L.C., attorneys for Defendant Charles Edward Greene.

> JONES, SKELTON & HOCHULI, P.L.C.
>
>
> By _____
> Robert R. Berk
> Suite 800
> 2901 North Central Avenue
> Phoenix, Arizona 85012
> Attorneys for Defendant Greene

William D. Holm, Bar #007412
Robert R. Berk, Bar #010162
JONES, SKELTON & HOCHULI, P.L.C.
2901 North Central Avenue, Suite 800
Phoenix, Arizona 85012
(602) 263-1700

Attorneys for Defendants Charles Edward Greene
 and Agnes Greene

SUPERIOR COURT OF THE STATE OF ARIZONA

COUNTY OF MARICOPA

MARK COCKRIEL,	NO. CV 2000-010963
Plaintiff,	
v.	**STIPULATED JUDGMENT**
ARIZONA CARDINALS, INC., an Arizona corporation; B&B HOLDINGS, INC., an Arizona corporation; CHARLES EDWARD GREENE (a/k/a MEAN JOE GREENE) and AGNES GREENE, husband and wife,	
Defendants.	(Assigned to Honorable William L. Topf, III)

Plaintiff Mark Cockriel and Defendant Charles Edward Greene, having entered into a Settlement Agreement, and Plaintiff and Defendant Charles Edward Greene having further stipulated to the entry of Judgment,

IT IS HEREBY ORDERED, ADJUDGED AND DECREED that on Count Five of Plaintiff's Amended Complaint, Judgment is entered in favor of Plaintiff and against Defendant Charles Edward Greene in the principal amount of $100,000.

IT IS FURTHER ORDERED that Plaintiff's remaining claims against Defendant Charles Edward Greene are dismissed with prejudice.

IT IS FURTHER ORDERED that there is no reason for the delay of entry of judgment, and the Clerk of the Court is directed to enter the same forthwith.

JONES, SKELTON & HOCHULI, P.L.C.
ATTORNEYS AT LAW
2901 NORTH CENTRAL AVENUE
SUITE 800
PHOENIX, ARIZONA 85012
TELEPHONE (602) 263-1700

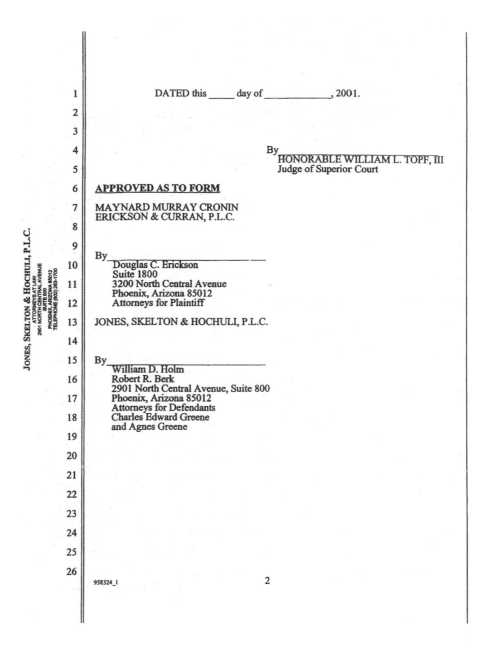

DATED this _____ day of _____, 2001.

By_____
HONORABLE WILLIAM L. TOPF, III
Judge of Superior Court

APPROVED AS TO FORM

MAYNARD MURRAY CRONIN
ERICKSON & CURRAN, P.L.C.

By_____
Douglas C. Erickson
Suite 1800
3200 North Central Avenue
Phoenix, Arizona 85012
Attorneys for Plaintiff

JONES, SKELTON & HOCHULI, P.L.C.

By_____
William D. Holm
Robert R. Berk
2901 North Central Avenue, Suite 800
Phoenix, Arizona 85012
Attorneys for Defendants
Charles Edward Greene
and Agnes Greene

JONES, SKELTON & HOCHULI, P.L.C.
ATTORNEYS AT LAW
SUITE 800
2901 NORTH CENTRAL AVENUE
PHOENIX, ARIZONA 85012
TELEPHONE (602) 263-1700

958324_1   2

QUESTIONS

1. How did Mark choose $100,000 in damages? Were there any limits on what amount Mark could have chosen?

2. Paragraph 4A of the agreement requires Joe to "reasonably cooperate" with the plaintiff in future proceedings. What does this mean, exactly?

3. Should the parties contemplating a Damron agreement be required to give notice to an insurance company that has failed to provide a defense?

4. Should a stipulated judgment be enough to form the basis of a Damron agreement? What about the possibility of collusion between the plaintiff and defendant in the underlying tort suit? This question is answered differently in different jurisdictions. Compare Iowa's answer in *Red Giant*, above, with Smith v. State Farm Mutual Automobile Ins. Co., in which a California appellate court held that a stipulated judgment could not form the basis of an enforceable Damron agreement unless there was other proof of the defendant's liability and amount of damages, such as a litigated judgment that occurs before the agreement between the plaintiff and defendant. In the *Smith* case, the court upheld the agreement based on a criminal conviction resulting from a jury trial related to the same incident. Even though the court ultimately held the agreement enforceable because of the criminal conviction, the court specifically noted that the amount of damages in the stipulated judgment should have no bearing on the amount of damages in the plaintiff's suit against the defendant's insurance company for bad faith refusal to defend. 7 Cal. Rptr. 2d 131 (Cal. Ct. App. 1992).

PART E: THE FIFTH QUARTER

The stipulated judgment and settlement agreement mark the end of the suit for Joe. Thanks to the agreement, Mark held a judgment that he could not execute against Joe personally. He began a second suit against Farmers for wrongly refusing to defend Joe, using Joe's now-assigned claim. (Can you think of a reason why Mark did not sue Gulf as well?)

Because Mark was hoping to collect from Joe's insurance company, it was imperative that his claim be one that is covered by the insurance coverage. As a result, Mark's initial theory of the case had to change from one of intentional tort to one of negligence. To pursue his claim against the insurance companies, Mark amended his original complaint to include a claim of negligence against Joe. Mark's motion to amend the complaint was submitted to the court at the same time as the motion for stipulated judgment, and Joe's attorneys raised no objection. The amended complaint included all the claims in the original complaint, but added the following negligence claim.

1   **<u>COUNT FIVE</u>**

2   **(Negligence)**

3   22.   Cockriel incorporates the allegations contained in paragraphs 1-21 as though

4 fully set forth herein.

5   23.   At a minimum, if not deliberate or intentional, the acts of Greene, as described

6 above, were negligent or reckless.

7   24.   At all pertinent times, Greene was acting within the scope of his employment.

8   25.   As a direct and proximate result of Greene's conduct, Cockriel suffered injuries.

9   WHEREFORE, Cockriel prays for judgment against all Defendants as follows:

10   A.   For compensatory damages in an amount to be proven at trial;

11   B.   For interest, costs and expenses incurred herein; and

12   C.   For such other and further relief as the Court deems just and proper.

Farmers moved for summary judgment, with two main arguments in defense. The first was that the initial decision to refuse coverage was correct — Joe's insurance policy did not cover the incident, so the carrier was not legally obligated to provide a defense or to indemnify Joe. In making this argument, Farmers made the same arguments regarding the exclusion of intentional acts from coverage, noting that the negligence claim only became a part of the complaint when the Damron agreement was entered. They also argued that the incident was not covered because it occurred during Joe's "business pursuits," which are excluded from coverage under the homeowner's policy.

Mark's attorney pointed out that the only evidence on the record bearing on intentional versus negligent acts was from Joe's deposition, reproduced in Chapter 2 — and that deposition squarely supported a negligence theory — and that the Cardinals were let out of the case precisely because Joe's actions were *not* thought to be within the scope of his employment. (An act might be argued to be a "business pursuit" even while not within the employee's "scope of employment"; these are the sort of details that a court has to sort out in reconciling the language of insurance contracts with related tort doctrine.)

The insurer's second argument was that the stipulated judgment in the case was "unreasonable," in part because it was the product of an agreement between Mark and Joe to the detriment of the insurance company. Farmers characterized the agreement as "collusive," noting that it was not given notice of the amended complaint. Farmers argued that the agreement is particularly unreasonable because it was entered only on the negligence count: "Given the egregiousness of Mr. Greene's conduct, it is possible that he and his counsel believed that the battery and punitive damage claim presented a six figure exposure. Nevertheless, the stipulated judgment was entered only on the negligence count. An accidental injury of the nature and extent described above [a total actual medical cost of only $285.00] does not constitute a claim worth $100,000."[4]

QUESTIONS

1. How would you have ruled on Farmers' motion for summary judgment, and why?
2. With the benefit of hindsight, is there anything the parties or the insurance companies should have done differently?

Farmers won its summary judgment motion in the trial court, and Mark appealed. Of central interest to the appellate court was whether indeed the record developed by the depositions could — construed most favorably to Mark — show that Joe did *not* act intentionally, thereby refuting Farmers' claim that the incident was outside the scope of its policy.

At the time of the depositions, Mark was himself proceeding on an intentional tort theory, and Mark's attorney was thus doing his utmost to push Joe during Joe's deposition to admit to an intentional act. It is helpful to review, as the court did, the deposition extracts found on pp. 22-30 of Chapter 2. They largely show Joe sticking to his explanation of himself as "just reacting" and acting "instinctively," along with the confusing statement, "I — I can say I did not intend not to hit him." (Such a statement could well be transcription error by the court reporter who attended the deposition. While lawyers from all parties are given a chance to augment a transcript with notes or claims of error after the transcript is prepared, no changes appear to have been made here.)

As the attorneys bicker over whether more questions should be permitted on this subject or whether they've already been asked and answered, Joe's lawyer — perhaps trying to fend off further probing in this area — is recorded as saying that "he's testified that he did it spontaneously and instinctively. The follow-up questions were, 'Was that accidental or intentional?' The answer to that question is already presumed within the spontaneous and instinctive answer."

As we have seen, thanks to the Damron agreement, by the time of Mark's case against Farmers, it is in Mark's interest to agree wholeheartedly with Joe's statements and to construe them as indications of unintentional behavior, as Joe's own lawyers sought to do. The table on pp. 64-65 of Chapter 2 draws from the Second Restatement of Torts to suggest that a "mere reflex" cannot constitute an act. The appellate court cited Joe's answers in his deposition — including the

---

[4] Defendant's Motion for Summary Judgment at 15, Cockriel v. Farmers Insurance Company (No. CV2002-009022, Superior Court of the State of Arizona, Maricopa County).

confusing answer ("I can say I did not intend not to hit him") — to conclude that a spontaneous or even instinctive act may still be more than reflexive, and that Joe's answers do not explicitly claim "reflex." The court wrote, "Merely because an action is spontaneous or unplanned does not make it involuntary, reflexive or otherwise unintentional. . . . [A]ccepting Greene's conduct as spontaneous, nothing in the record suggests that his action was an involuntary or physiological reflex or that his mental condition 'deprive[d] him of the capacity to act rationally and therefore negate[d] the deliberateness of his "intentional" injury-causing act.'"[5]

Had Joe's deposition gone in a slightly different direction, the appeals court might have come out the other way, or at least invoked other reasons to preclude recovery by Mark against Farmers. On the basis of those answers, however, the appeals court affirmed the trial court's judgment, effectively ending the case in favor of Farmers.

QUESTIONS

1. In retrospect, if Mark's lawyer were redoing the deposition, what might he change in his questions?

2. Why would Joe repeatedly describe his actions as spontaneous and instinctive, but pointedly not characterize them as either accidental or intentional? (Indeed, his lawyer's recorded objection says that the answer to the "accidental or intentional?" question is "already presumed" in Joe's earlier characterizations — without himself suggesting what that presumed answer is. Apparently because of that objection, Joe never firmly went on record one way or the other with an explicit answer.)

3. Reread the three questions (and answers) in Joe's deposition on p. 33. Do Joe's answers support the notion of a spontaneous yet deliberate act?

4. The tap of a doctor's hammer upon one's knee is often cited as a canonically reflexive — and therefore unintentional — act. Perhaps according to the table on pp. 64-65 it would not even rise to the level of an "act," intentional or otherwise. What about swatting at a bee that buzzes around one's head while driving? Are there other examples that can help refine categories into which the incident upon which this book is based might fall?

5. How important did the doctrinal nuances of assault and battery turn out to be to the resolution of Mark's case against Joe? Against Farmers?

---

[5] Memorandum Decision, *Cockriel v. Farmers Insurance Company of Arizona* (No. CA-CV 03-0381, Court of Appeals, State of Arizona), March 30, 2004, ¶ 18.